THE

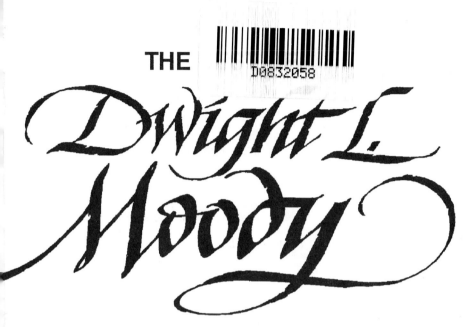

Dwight L. Moody

Edited by
Ralph Turnbull

BAKER BOOK HOUSE
Grand Rapids, Michigan

Copyright © 1971 by Baker Books
a division of Baker Book House Company
P.O. Box 6287, Grand Rapids, MI 49516-6287

ISBN: 0-8010-6216-0

Sixth printing, October 1995

Formerly published under the title
The Treasury of Dwight L. Moody

Printed in the United States of America

Contents

INTRODUCTION

In the roster of evangelists and preachers Dwight Lyman Moody (1837-1899) stands high for the impact of his ministry in the English-speaking world. A New Englander of humble origin, he lived a full life as a salesman and then as a salesman for God. He came at the end of the evangelical period of influence in America when liberalism was emerging. His minstry had the support and backing of people in both movements and the whole church was influenced and blessed through his forthright preaching. Moody moved freely in both America and in Great Britain among men of different theological views and united them in the work of evangelism. Out of his efforts and influence many united movements were stimulated to practical action. The Y.M.C.A., the American Sunday School Union, the American Tract Society, the American Bible Society, Moody Tract and Colportage Association, the Moody Memorial Church, Chicago; The Moody Bible Institute of Chicago; the Northfield and Mount Hermon Schools for Boys and Girls, Mount Hermon, Massachusetts, are among many in the United States. In Great Britain came several large mission agencies as the Tent Hall, Glasgow; Carrubbers Close Mission, Edinburgh; and the Bible Training Institute, Glasgow. Movements of unity and united action were areas in which he worked with Christians of all backgrounds in seeking to reach the lost of his generation.

In religious conviction and theological background, Moody, from his conversion and subsequent deepened spiritual experience by the Holy Spirit's indwelling, was an avowed evangelical. In his closing years he was associated with those who were aligning in the more fundamentalist movement then crystalizing. It is significant that whereas he was for many years spoken of and written about by sympathetic and eulogistic friends, the more recent biographies and studies have come from those of more critical affinities. For half a century and more only eulogistic "lives" were written. Now the greater wealth of sources available to the historian, the writer, and the biographer have given us a truer picture of this amazing personality. We begin to understand that we cannot assess the social and religious life of America from 1870 and on unless we give sympathetic examination of Moody's life and work. The most recent and the best study of D. L. Moody has come out of the context of the University of Chicago, and its appraisal is definitive and balanced in its judgment. Moody now is seen as one of most creative influences in the United States from the 1870's by his preaching and ministry.

As a lay evangelist Moody was in the succession of many across the centuries and from Biblical times. He would not be associated with the impassioned Isaiah or the eloquent Apollos: he was closer to the rugged Amos and the blunt Peter. The wisdom of Moses and the education of Paul were not his: he had another endowment like the loving compassion of Hosea and the pin-pointed speech of Matthew the business man. His early years in business and as a shoe salesman prepared him to meet and approach people directly with the gospel. In the Chicago Sunday School work and the service given to the soldiers in the Civil War as a lay minister, he laid the foundation of later evangelistic efforts. He was not the product of a theological seminary or a college education, but when he spoke he was heard like his Lord and Master of whom it was said: "whence has this man letters, having never learned?" and "the common people heard him gladly."

His sermons of which this Treasury is a sampling were simple and to the point. They lack homiletical structure, but were well illustrated for contact with people of all walks of life.

Moody did not hesitate to borrow freely from others in what was said or written if it assisted him with his message. This was not "plagiarism" in the ordinary sense, but a desire to "learn from others" because of his earlier limited education. Anyone who had something worthwhile to say would find him at their feet to listen and learn. The messages for the most part were taken down verbatim by eager newspaper reporters who followed him and found good "copy" for the press. He stood sturdy and stocky in build, with unmusical voice, but with earnest and compassionate tones pleading with people.

The sermons have no literary merit or polished style of any school. They carry the thrust of brusk, straight-forward utterance. The common touch and the homely story found entrance into the mind of simple, common people, but also was received by the educated who overlooked the blemishes of speech of this salesman for God. Sometimes and more than the exception, the sermons were diffuse, rambling, unconnected, and repetitious. Logical structure was lacking as in a Charles G. Finney, the lawyer-evangelist before him, but in spite of these handicaps Moody stirred the crowds by his sincereity and zeal. Dr. R. W. Dale, eminent Congregational preacher-theologian in England, supported Moody and said of him: "he was the only man he knew who could speak of hell — he had tears when he spoke!" He also called attention to the evangelistic emphasis of the evangelist on "Christ as Mediator": "that Christ came to save men, and can do it, is the substance of nearly all of his discourses."

When an appraisal of Moody's Theology is attempted, we find him preaching on the major themes of evangelicalism — "sin — salvation — power of the Holy Spirit — Christ's death and resurrection — (little about the Incarnation) — " with strong proclamation concerning the Atonement. He accepted the historic view of the vicarious and substitutionary death of Christ. His preaching was not bound by any systematic views he may have inherited from others he heard in his formative years. His constant and concentrated Bible study was the foundation of his belief. The stress here is obviously on what is known as "the moral influence" theory of the Atonement. It was the vicarious nature of Christ's death which moved him to say: "because He died for me, I love Him. Because He died for me, I will serve Him. I will work for Him, I will give Him my very life."

His messages were Christ-centered and Moody was wont to say: "that faith isn't a creed about Christ, but it is Christ." This personal encounter was at the heart of his appeal for decision and discipleship. Moody found in his day that faith in God and general acceptance of the Bible made it easy for him to urge a commitment. He saw that a time was coming (our day) that there would be a decay of such faith and then we would need a *teaching* evangelism. His work was made much simpler in that the background of belief and instruction was there and he had only to call to decision. Thus his influence was widespread. A study of social movements during the 1870's and '90s would bring to light that Moody was not only in the mainstream of American religious fundamentalism, but was closer to that part of evangelicalism which was then profoundly influenced by British pietistic biblicism. The stress on God's love for man's salvation was closer to Methodist (not Congregational) theology. His own spiritual awakening and deepening of faith at the crucial juncture of his ministry had links with the piety and search for perfection then in vogue.

In preparing this Treasury I recall that my first introduction to D. L. Moody was the mention of his name repeatedly in religious circles in Edinburgh, Scotland. I was a lad just committed to Christ and engaged in evangelistic work with other young men. Those who led us told how this American layman had come to our city and country, and under God was used to stir the churches and reach to the public without. The results of his work were around us in churches and missions where men spoke of him with respect and thanksgiving. Dr. George H. Morrison, in his Moderator's message given at the General Assembly of the United Free Church of Scotland, in the Assembly Hall, Edinburgh, on the subject of "Revival" paid eloquent testimony to the ministry of Moody. Listening as a student I recall he said that "looking back over his lifetime and surveying the church life of Scotland, more pastors and elders owed their salvation and spiritual awakening to the work of Moody than to any other influence." Thus the tradition of an enlightened evangelical ministry has continued in that land.

Moody's many published volumes have been consulted and from these a selection has been made to cover a wide variety of his preaching and teaching. The Bibliography indicates many of these sources. No one can say with certitude what was the secret of this man's life and work. His limitations in education were obvious. His handicaps as far as worldly success was measured were not hidden. To engage in the preaching ministry as a lay evangelist in a day when in America and in Great Britain there were scores of outstanding preachers whose names were household names was from a human judgment — foolishness. Yet in the divine providence this was the man matched for that hour whom God chose to use — "the treasure in an earthen vessel" (II Cor. 4:7).

Several significant words should be noted:

Robert W. Dale, Birmingham, England, was puzzled because of the ordinary man with lack of distinctive power, yet holding thousands of people enthralled with gospel preaching. Once he remarked to Moody rather bluntly that "the work was most plainly of God, for I could see no real relation between him and what he had done."

Henry Varley, West London, England, spoke casually on one occasion and the words startled Moody: "the world has yet to see what God can do with and for and through a man who is fully and wholy consecrated to Him." In reflection, Moody said "a man! He meant *any* man. He didn't say he had to be educated, or brilliant, or anything else. Just a *man*. Well, by the Holy Spirit in me I'll be that man."

G. Campbell Morgan paid tribute to Moody as "a man sent from God" with an octagon of strength. In that eightfold character manifested in *him* was — "tenderness, humor, common sense, insight, immediateness, passion, breadth, and modesty."

Henry Drummond said of Moody, "He was the biggest human I ever met."

To those of us who did not live in Moody's day or have that privilege of hearing him preach, a Treasury in writing may well be an introduction to the mind and spirit of one of God's radiant servants. He was a special instrument chosen by God. It would be utterly foolish to say that anyone could have done, or that anyone could do now the work that Moody did. He was given to the church, and through the church to the world at a time when there was the need of the gospel of the grace of God. The selections could carry the flame from that living fire of yesterday to stir some new blaze today.

RALPH G. TURNBULL

The First Presbyterian Church
of Seattle, Washington, 1970

THE BEST OF

THE PRECIOUS BLOOD

In I Peter 1:18, we read: "Forasmuch as ye know that ye were not redeemed with corruptible things, as silver and gold, from your vain conversation, received by tradition from your fathers, but with the precious blood of Christ, as of a lamb without blemish and without spot."

Peter was an old man when he wrote those words. I suppose the blood of Jesus grew more precious to him as the years went by.

IT REDEEMS

Now, why is it precious? First, because *it redeems us*. Not only from the hands of the devil, but from the hands of the law. It redeems me from the curse of the law; it brings me out from under the law. The law condemns me, but Christ has satisfied the claims of the law. He tasted death for every man, and He has made it possible for every man to be saved. Paul says, God gave Him up freely for us all, and what we want to do is to take Him.

Silver and gold could not redeem our souls. Our life had been forfeited. Death had come into the world by sin, and nothing but blood could atone for the soul. If gold and silver could have redeemed us, do you not think that God would have created millions of worlds full of gold? It would have been an easy matter for Him. But we are not redeemed by such corruptible things, but by the precious blood of Christ. Redemption means

15

"buying back"; we had sold ourselves for naught, and Christ redeemed us and bought us back.

A friend in Ireland once met a little Irish boy who had caught a sparrow. The poor little bird was trembling in his hand, and seemed very anxious to escape. The gentleman begged the boy to let it go, as the bird could not do him any good; but the boy said he would not, for he had chased it three hours before he could catch it. He tried to reason it out with the boy, but it vain. At last he offered to buy the bird. The boy agreed to the price, and it was paid. Then the gentleman took the poor little thing, and held it out on his hand. The boy had been holding it very fast, for the boy was stronger than the bird, just as Satan is stronger than we; and there it sat for a time scarcely able to realize the fact that it had got liberty; but in a little it flew away chirping, as if to say to the gentleman: "Thank you! thank you! you have redeemed me."

This is what redemption is — buying back and setting free. Christ came to break the fetters of sin, to open the prison doors and set the sinner free.

IT BLOTS OUT SIN

It is precious, because *it blots out sin*. Thank God for that! You see a cloud, and it is gone soon into vapor and disappears; can it ever be found in the history of the world? Never. There may be other clouds, but that cloud will never appear again. A child writes on his slate, and then rubs the writing out. Where is it gone? It can not be found. Can any of your modern philosophers find it? And so does the blood of Jesus Christ blot out sin. There was a woman in Ireland they were telling about when I was over there, that had a little class in school; and she asked if there was anything that God couldn't do. And one little child said, "Yes, He can't see my sins through the blood of Jesus Christ." That is what He cannot do. The blood just blots out.

I believe that when we get to heaven we will find men whom we have known to be thieves and drunkards and murderers, men as black and vile as any men that ever trod this earth, as pure as the Son of God, because the blood of Jesus Christ has made them clean. And so any man or woman in this wide world who is steeped in the blackest kind of sin, can be as white as a lily by the blood of Jesus Christ.

IT BRINGS US NIGH

Another thing: *the blood brings us nigh.*

"But now in Christ Jesus ye who sometimes were far off are made nigh by the blood of Christ" (Eph. 2:13).

It not only brings us near to God, but brings us near to one another. I can go to any community where I am an entire stranger, and preach this doctrine of atonement, and get better acquainted in twenty-four hours than I could if I talked about old Socrates and Plato for twenty-four years. The blood brings us nigh; we realize that we are "blood relatives." The tie is stronger than any natural tie. If a church got divided and I wanted to bring them together, what I would do would be to preach Christ. Hold up the cross, and you will get the true believers around it in a little while; but go to preaching science and botany and astronomy and metaphysics, and you will get them all quarreling. The cross is the drawing power. The cross is the center. Bring people nigh to it and you bring them nigh to each other.

Let some one die, and see how quickly the family will come together. So we gather around the cross where Christ died for me and for you. That brings us nigh; I am a blood relative of yours.

IT MAKES PEACE

The blood is precious because *it makes peace.* "Having made peace through the blood of the cross" (Col. 1:20).

You can look for peace the world over, and you will never

find it until you get to the cross. You haven't got to make it; it is already made. Did you ever think, when Christ died, He made out His will? Perhaps you thought you had never been mentioned in any will. Well, you have, if you are a child of God. When Christ was on the cross, He made out His will. He willed His spirit back to His Father; He willed His body to Joseph of Arimathea; He willed His mother to John the son of Zebedee; and then to His disciples He said, "Peace I leave with you; My peace I give unto you." Joy and peace were His legacies. Pretty good legacies, weren't they? You can have them if you will.

They say now-a-days that they can't make a will that is so sure that some keen lawyer can't smash it all to pieces; but I challenge any man to break Christ's will. He rose to execute His own will. Neither man or devil can break it. He made peace by His blood on the cross.

I want to say very emphatically that I do not believe there is a man or woman on this earth who knows what peace of conscience and peace of mind and peace of soul are who doesn't know the doctrine of the atonement. I do not believe there is a spot where peace can be found except under the shadow of the cross. The billows may come surging and rolling up against us, but if we find refuge and shelter under the cross of Jesus Christ we have peace.

Do you want peace? Is your soul tossed on the waves of trouble and sorrow and persecution? If you do, my friends, just get hold of this doctrine.

During the last days of the civil war, when many men were deserting from the South, Secretary Stanton sent out a notice from the War Department that no more refugees be taken into the Union army. A Southern soldier hadn't seen that, and he came into the Union lines and they read the order to him. He didn't know what to do. If he went back into the Southern army he would be shot as a deserter, and the Northern army wouldn't have him. So he went into the woods between the armies and stayed until he got starved out. He saw an officer going by, and he rushed out of the woods and told this officer that if he didn't help him he would have to take his life. The officer asked what was the trouble. He told him. The officer said:

"Haven't you heard the news?"

"No, what news?"

"Why, the war is over. Lee has surrendered. Peace is declared. Go to the first town, and get all the food you want."

The man waved his hat and went to the town as quick as he could.

I want to say that peace is declared, the war is over. Be ye reconciled to God, and the whole thing is settled. The trouble is on your side. The blood is on the mercy seat, and as long as it is there the vilest sinner can enter and be saved for time and eternity.

IT JUSTIFIES

It is precious, because *it justifies me*. "Being now justified by His blood we shall be saved from wrath through Him" (Rom. 5:9).

I haven't been able to climb up to the height of that word "justified." Do you know what it means? It is better than pardon. Justification means that there isn't a charge against you. Your sins are completely wiped out; they are not to be remembered; they are not to be mentioned. Think of it! God says He puts them out of His memory. In other words, I have been running up an account down at the grocery store for some years, and I haven't any money to pay. I go down there, and the storekeeper says:

"Mr. Moody, I have good news for you. A friend of yours came here to-day and paid the whole bill; it is all settled."

That is justification. "Who shall lay anything to the charge of God's elect? God that justifieth?" He won't do it; He would be a strange judge if He justified a man and then brought a charge against him. "Who is he that condemneth? Christ that died, yea, rather that is risen again?" Thank God for the precious blood which justifies me. No wonder when that truth dawned on Martin Luther, he rose and he shook all Europe.

IT CLEANSES

It is precious because *it cleanses me*. "If we walk in the light, as He is in the light, we have fellowship one with another, and the blood of Jesus Christ His Son cleanseth us from all sin" (I John 1:7).

The blood of Jesus Christ cleanses from all sin. Think of it. Not a part of our sin, but ALL. We Christians ought to be the happiest people in the world.

IT GIVES BOLDNESS

And it is precious because it is going to *give me boldness in the day of judgment*. Isn't that good?

Do you know I pity these people who live all their life-time under the bondage of death. If I am behind the blood of the Son of God, judgment is already passed; it is behind me; it is not before me. Know ye not that ye shall judge the world? People live in constant dread of the great white throne judgment. When that comes, I am going to be with Christ on the throne, I am not going to be judged! That day is passed to the true child of God. "He was wounded for our transgressions, He was bruised for our iniquities," and is God going to demand payment twice? I am going to have boldness in the day of judgment.

There is a story of a man who was going to be tried for his life, and if found guilty there was no hope for him unless the king would intercede. They went to the king, and he finally consented to give a pardon, but he said:

"Let it be secret, and if the man isn't condemned, do not say anything about it; if he is condemned, he can use the pardon."

The man went into court with the pardon in his pocket, and he was quite cheerful about his trial. It went against him, and when the judge pronounced the sentence upon him, he took pains to say that he and the whole court were shocked to think that a man could be on trial for his life and be so unconcerned.

When the judge got through, the man stepped up and laid the king's pardon on the judge's desk, and walked out bold as a lion.

You have a charge against me. What do I care? God has justified me. He comes and says, "Moody, you are a saved man." Yes, saved by grace, saved for time and for eternity.

JESUS FULFILLING PROPHECY

You THAT were here last Sunday morning remember I was speaking about Christ in the Old Testament, and how the Scripture was fulfilled in his birth. This morning I want to take up the subject where I left off, and show that everything about Christ was wonderful. All these prophecies in the Old Testament about Christ were wonderful; everything about his life and death were wonderful. We find a great many people now who tell us that they don't see anything wonderful in Christ; that he was like ordinary men, like all other men; and they see no reason why they should believe in him as being more than human. I want to call your attention to what Gabriel said about him.

Gabriel's name appears three times in Scripture; and every time that he comes to earth, he comes to bring some tidings about the Lord Jesus Christ. He first came to Babylon, when Daniel was praying, to tell him that he was not only greatly beloved, but to give him the secret that was in heaven: that the Messiah should come, and that he should be cut off for the transgressions of God's people. Five hundred years have rolled away, and the last prophet's voice has been heard in the land and the Word has been sealed; his prophecy has been closed, and not a sound of a prophet has been heard in that land that had been so exalted. The last prophecy was closed up about four hundred years before Christ came; and an old priest by the name of Zacharias was burning incense in the Temple, in his regular course. We are told that he and his wife Elizabeth were good people; they were righteous, but they had a crook in their path like a great many now. They had no children, and it was considered in those days a great dishonor not to have children; and we are told that they had been praying that they might have a child; but I suppose they had grown faint, and had given up all hope of having their prayers answered; perhaps they had forgotten how God answered the prayers of Abraham and Sarah and gave them a child in their old age, and how Hannah also had a child in her old age, and also how Samson's father and mother had been honored by a child. And now we find that this old priest was not in the holiest of the holies, but in the place where they burned incense, just outside of the curtain that was rent when Christ died. There was an altar, and on it was the incense, where he went in twice a day to burn the incense to God; and while he was thus engaged, the people were in the outer court; and it was the custom for them to wait until the priest came out, and I suppose he blessed them, the same as people wait now for the benediction, — although they don't always wait here, but hurry to get home some nights; but in those days they waited for the benediction. And the old priest didn't come out one day, he tarried longer than usual; for while he was thus engaged at the altar who should meet him but this same man Gabriel, who met Daniel away off in Babylon five hundred years before, and Zacharias was filled with fear when he saw him; and he told him to fear not, he brought him some good news; his prayers were answered. Let me read what Gabriel said to the old priest:

"And there appeared unto him an angel of the Lord, standing on the right side of the altar of incense. And when Zacharias saw him he was troubled and fear fell upon him. But the angel said unto him, fear not, Zachariah; for thy prayer is heard: and thy wife, Elizabeth, shall bear thee a son, and thou shalt call his name John. And thou shalt have joy and gladness, and many shall rejoice at his birth. For he shall be great in the sight of the

Lord, and shall drink neither wine nor strong drink; and he shall be filled with the Holy Ghost, even from his mother's womb. And many of the children of Israel shall be turn to the Lord their God. And he shall go before him in the spirit and power of Elias, to turn the hearts of the fathers toward the children, and the disobedient to the wisdom of the just; to make ready a people prepared for the Lord." He was not only to have a child, but his child was to become great in the sight of God; and he was not only to become great, but to become a good child, and to be filled with the Holy Ghost from the womb, and he should turn many to righteousness.

How pleased that old priest was; but Zacharias was like a great many now, full of unbelief. Instead of remembering how God had answered the prayers of Abraham, he says, "How can this be? how can I have a child?" "And Zacharias said unto the angel, Whereby shall I know this? for I am an old man, and my wife well stricken in years. And the angel answering, said unto him, I am Gabriel, that stand in the presence of God." I suppose Gabriel never had been doubted before. He might have said, "Where has an angel ever told a lie?" An angel sent by God into this world never told a lie; and all the promises they brought to this world have been literally fulfilled. He was amazed, perhaps for the first time in his life. He had come from a world where unbelief is a stranger, where doubts are unknown; where everyone believes what God has said; and now he thinks that this old priest ought to have known what God said was true. But Zacharias wanted a token. Somebody has said that is the trouble now in the churches; a great many people want a token, outside the Word of God. Gabriel said, "You shall have a token, you shall be dumb for the next nine months; you shall not speak until the child is born." He got all the token he wanted. The reason we have so many dumb Christians is, they want a token, outside of the Bible, and they are not sure what God says is true. When he came out, the people noticed a change in the old priest; and there was no small stir in Jerusalem, when it was written out by Zacharias what had taken place. When the time came for him to retire from office, he took his wife and went off in the hilly country of Judea; and he remained until the child was born.

But six months from that time Gabriel made his third visit. Gabriel came down again, and he brought better news than ever. He came to that country girl off in Nazareth, and tells her that she is to be the mother of that child that Israel had been looking for, for 4,000 years. Wonder of wonders! No wonder that she was startled; all the mothers in Israel had been praying that they might be the mother of that child. Here is a young country girl, a young virgin, that was to be the mother of that child. Let us read what Gabriel says to her: "And in the sixth month, the angel Gabriel was sent from God unto a city of Galilee named Nazareth; to a virgin espoused to a man whose name was Joseph, of the house of David, and the virgin's name was Mary. And the angel came in unto her and said, Hail thou that art highly favored, the Lord is with thee; blessed art thou among women. And when she saw him she was troubled at his saying, and cast in her mind what manner of salutation this should be. And the angel said unto her, Fear not, Mary, for thou hast found favor with God. And behold thou shalt conceive in thy womb and bring forth a son, and shall call his name Jesus. He shall be great, and shall be called the Son of the Highest; and the Lord God shall give unto him the throne of his father David. And he shall reign over the house of Jacob forever; and of his kingdom there shall be no end."

How that has been fulfilled. Eighteen hundred years have rolled away; he has got a kingdom in this world; it is in the hearts of many. There are millions this morning that would go to the stake to lay down their lives for this kingdom, for Christ; there are many loyal sons to-day in the world; loyal to the King of Heaven.

"Then said Mary unto the angel, How shall this be seeing I know not a man? And the angel answered and said unto her: The Holy Ghost shall come upon thee, and the power of the highest shall overshadow thee; therefore also that holy thing which shall be born of thee shall be called the Son of God. And behold thy cousin Elizabeth, she hath also conceived a son in her old age; and this is the sixth month with her who was called barren. For with God nothing shall be impossible." Bear in mind what Gabriel said to Mary about this child. He was not only to be great, but his name should be great, too; He shall be called Jesus. He has 256 names, which you can find in the Bible; but he still bears that name; we like it better than any other. It was the name which came from heaven; it was the sweetest name any mortal had; it was the name which fired up the whole Jewish nation, like Joshua's. They ought to have hailed it with joy and gladness; they had got another Joshua, another deliverer, one who was come to set the captives free, as we have been trying to tell you this past week. Mary started at once, left her home in Nazareth and went off into the hill country where Elizabeth was; and the moment she met that aged cousin of hers, that child leaped in the womb. Marvelous and wonderful thing! And yet men say they don't see anything wonderful about it. Everything about Christ is wonderful. And now we find that Elizabeth breaks out into praise, and so does Mary.

I wish I had time to read what they said, but they spent three months together, and just before John is born Mary returns to her own country; and it seems to me quite singular that this last prophet that was to be given to the old nation — the old dispensation was just fading away, just dying out, and they were right on the eve of a new dispensation — that John should be born of an old woman, but Christ, who was to usher in the new, was to be born of a young virgin. And in the fullness of time, when the nine months had expired, John was born; and his relatives wanted to call him after his father, but Elizabeth insisted on calling him John. Finally they asked the old priest, and he wrote, "His name shall be called John." That name came from heaven. Gabriel brought the name John, and they could not have changed it. In the 65th verse of the 1st chapter of Luke it says: "And fear came on all that dwelt round about there; and all these sayings were noised abroad throughout the hill-country of Judea. And all they that heard them laid them up in their hearts, saying, What manner of child shall this be? And the hand of the Lord was with him."

John means the grace of God! This was the grace of God, giving us this child; and about three months from that time there was another stir at Bethlehem — Mary gave birth to the child Jesus. The shepherds made haste to find the child, and when they found it they made haste to proclaim him to the world.

"And when eight days were accomplished for the circumcising of the child, his name was called JESUS, which was so named of the angel before he was conceived in the womb." In another place it says: "His name shall be called JESUS, for he shall save his people from their sins." Let me ask you if it is true; will He save His people from their sins? Can a man save another man from sin? Would you say that there is another man in the world that can save this world from sin? Suppose we began to preach up some other man, eleven weeks ago; do you think there would have been so many people here this morning? What other name can we preach? Now just think a moment. Suppose we preach anything but Jesus Christ; would this crowd have been here this morning? Could they have been held together for eleven weeks? This very fact, it seems to me, ought to settle this question who Christ is. You may preach other names; but that will not save men from sin. You may preach that people ought to be moral and virtuous and ought to do this and do that; but if you don't tell them where they can get the power from to do it, they will go right on in their sins. But the moment you begin to preach Christ, and tell the world that He has power on earth to forgive sins, and "His name shall be called Jesus for He shall save his people from their sins," why then the people begin to gather to him. And where is there a name to be compared with that of Jesus? See how his kingdom is being extended, and how the heralds of the cross are going over deserts and mountains, and over this dark earth, to proclaim his name to a perishing world.

But then another scene takes place, we find them in the temple. "And behold, there was a man in Jerusalem, whose name was Simeon; and the same man was just and devout, waiting for the consolation of Israel; and the Holy Ghost was upon him." I want to call your attention to one thought, that whenever the Holy Ghost is upon a man he will always honor Christ and speak well of him. "And it was revealed unto him, by the Holy Ghost, that he should not see death before he had seen the Lord's Christ. And he came by the Spirit into the temple; and when the parents brought in the child Jesus, to do for him after the customs of the law, then took he him up in his arms, and blessed God, and said, Lord, now lettest thou thy servant depart in peace, according to thy word; for mine eyes have seen thy salvation, which thou hast prepared before the face of all thy people; a light to lighten the Gentiles, and the glory of thy people Israel." That was prophetic. The light hadn't gone out then to the Gentiles; they were considered by the Jews outcasts; they were not allowed to go into their temple, only into the outer court. "And Joseph and his mother marveled at these things, which were spoken of him. And Simeon blessed them, and said unto Mary his mother, Behold, this child is set for the fall and rising again of many in Israel; and for a sign which shall be spoken against. Yet, a sword shall pierce through thine own soul also; that the thoughts of many hearts may be revealed." (Mr. Moody then read from the 35th to the 39th verses.)

Jerusalem is again startled; this time by the wise men coming from the East to see him that was born King of the Jews. They go to Nazareth, guided by the star, and worship that little babe as God. He was God in flesh, the son of God come down from heaven to redeem the world. Herod ordered all those little children to be put to death. They were the first martyrs; "for of such is the kingdom of Heaven." Herod the Great was the first enemy Christ had, the first to unsheath the sword again Christ; and history tells us that he only lived thirty days after unsheathing that sword. The stone fell upon him and crushed him to powder; and instead of his falling before the stone and yielding to Christ, he drew his sword against him and was going to find him; but God took care of his child and He was safe in Egypt when Herod's order was executed. Herod was called Herod the Great, but how small be looked; his name has gone down to posterity rotten.

Oh, may God help us this morning to hail the coming Christ. He is going to come back, by and by, and reign upon earth. May God help each one of us to receive him as our Redeemer.

THE CHRISTIAN'S WARFARE

I would like to have you open your Bible at the first epistle of John, fifth chapter, fourth and fifth verses: "Whatsoever is born of God overcometh the world: and this is the victory that overcometh the world, even our faith. Who is he that overcometh the world, but he that believeth that Jesus is the Son of God?"

When a battle is fought, all are anxious to know who are the victors. In these verses we are told who is to gain the victory in life. When I was converted I made this mistake: I thought the battle was already mine, the victory already won, the crown already in my grasp. I thought that old things had passed away, that all things had become new; that my old corrupt nature, the Adam life, was gone. But I found out, after serving Christ for a few months, that conversion was only like enlisting in the army, that there was a battle on hand, and that if I was to get a crown, I had to work for it and fight for it.

Salvation is a gift, as free as the air we breathe. It is to be obtained, like any other gift, without money and without price: there are no other terms. "To him that worketh not, but believeth." But on the other hand, if we are to gain a crown, we must work for it. Let me quote a few verses in First Corinthians: "For other foundation can no man lay than that which is laid, which is Jesus Christ. But if any man buildeth on the foundation gold, silver, costly stones, wood, hay, stubble; each man's work shall be made manifest: for the day shall declare it, because it is revealed in fire: and the fire itself shall prove each man's work, of what sort it is. If any man's work shall abide, which he built thereon, he shall receive a reward. If any man's work shall be burned, he shall suffer loss: but he himself shall be saved; yet so as through fire."

We see clearly from this that we may be saved, but all our works burned up. I may have a wretched, miserable voyage through life, with no victory, and no reward at the end; saved, yet so as by fire, or as Job puts it, "with the skin of my teeth." I believe that a great many men will barely get to heaven as Lot got out of Sodom, burned out, nothing left, works and everything else destroyed.

It is like this: when a man enters the army, he is a member of the army the moment he enlists; he is just as much a member as a man who has been in the army ten or twenty years. But enlisting is one thing, and participating in a battle another. Young converts are like those just enlisted.

It is folly for any man to attempt to fight in his own strength. The world, the flesh and the devil are too much for any man. But if we are linked to Christ by faith, and He is formed in us the hope of glory, then we shall get the victory over every enemy. It is believers who are the overcomers. "Thanks be unto God, which always causeth us to triumph in Christ." Through Him we shall be more than conquerors.

I wouldn't think of talking to unconverted men about overcoming the world, for it is utterly impossible. They might as well try to cut down the American forest with their penknives. But a good many Christian people make this mistake: they think the battle is already fought and won. They have an idea that all they have to do is to put the oars down in the bottom of the boat, and the current will drift them into the ocean of God's eternal love. But we have to cross the current. We have to learn how to watch and fight, and how to overcome. The battle is only just commenced. The Christian life as a conflict and a warfare, and the quicker we find it out the better. There is not a blessing in this world that God has not linked Himself to. All the great and higher blessings God associates with Himself. When God and man work together, then it is that there is going to be victory. We are co-workers with Him. You might take a mill, and put it forty feet above a river, and there isn't capital enough in the States to make that river turn the mill; but get it down about forty feet, and away it works. We want to keep in mind that if we are going to overcome the world, we have got to work with God. It is His power that makes all the means of grace effectual.

The story is told that Frederick Douglas, the great slave orator, once said in a mournful speech when things looked dark for his race:—

"The white man is against us, governments are against us, the spirit of the times is against us. I see no hope for the colored race. I am full of sadness."

Just then a poor old colored woman rose in the audience, and said.—

"Frederick, is God dead?"

My friend, it makes a difference when you count God in.

Now many a young believer is discouraged and disheartened when he realizes this warfare. He begins to think that God has forsaken him, that Christianity is not all that it professes to be. But he should rather regard it as an encouraging sign. No sooner has a soul escaped from his snare than the great Adversary takes steps to ensnare it again. He puts forth all his power to recapture his lost prey. The fiercest attacks are made on the strongest forts, and the fiercer the battle the young believer is called on to wage, the surer evidence it is of the work of the Holy Spirit in his heart. God will not desert him in his time of need, any more than He deserted His people of old when they were hard pressed by their foes.

THE ONLY COMPLETE VICTOR

This brings me to the fourth verse of the fourth chapter of the same epistle: "Ye are of God, little children, and have overcome them: because greater is He that is in you than he that is in the world." The only man that ever conquered this world — was complete victor — was Jesus Christ. When He shouted on the cross, "It is finished!" it was the shout of a conqueror. He had overcome every enemy. He had met sin and death. He had met every foe that you and I have got to meet, and had come off victor. Now if I have got the spirit of Christ, if I have got that same life in me, then it is that I have got a power that is greater than any power in the world, and with that same power I overcome the world.

Notice that everything human in this world fails. Every man the moment he takes his eye off God, has failed. Every man has been a failure at some period of his life. Abraham failed. Moses failed. Elijah failed. Take the men that have become so famous and that were so mighty — the moment they got their eye off God, they were weak like other men; and it is a very singular thing that those men failed on the strongest point in their character. I suppose it was because they were not on the watch. Abraham was noted for his faith, and he failed right there — he denied his wife. Moses was noted for his meekness and humility, and he failed right there — he got angry. God kept him out of the promised land because he lost his temper. I know he was called "the servant of God," and that he was a mighty man, and had power with God, but humanly speaking, he failed, and was kept out of the promised land. Elijah was noted for his power in prayer and for his courage, yet he became a coward. He was the boldest man of his day, and stood before Ahab, and the royal court, and all the prophets of Baal; yet when he heard that Jezebel had threatened his life, he ran away to the desert, and under a juniper tree prayed that he might die. Peter was noted for his boldness, and a little maid scared him nearly out of his wits. As soon as she spoke to him, he began to tremble, and he swore that he didn't know Christ. I have often said to myself that I'd like to have been there on the day of Pentecost alongside of that maid when she saw Peter preaching.

"Why," I suppose she said, "what has come over that man? He was afraid of *me* only a few weeks ago, and now he stands up before all Jerusalem and charges these very Jews with the murder of Jesus."

The moment he got his eye off the Master he failed; and every man, I don't care who he is — even the strongest — every man that hasn't Christ in him, is a failure. John, the beloved disciple, was noted for his meekness; and yet we hear of him wanting to call fire down from heaven on a little town because it had refused the common hospitalities.

TRIUMPHS OF FAITH

Now, how are we to get the victory over all our enemies? Turn to Galatians, second chapter, verse twenty: "I am crucified with Christ; nevertheless I live; yet not I, but Christ liveth in me: and the life which I now live in the flesh, I live by the faith of the Son of God, who loved me and gave Himself for me." We live by faith. We get this life by faith, and become linked to Immanuel — "God with us." If I have God for me, I am going to overcome. How do we gain this mighty power? by faith.

The next passage I want to call your attention to is Romans, chapter eleven, verse twenty: "Because of unbelief they were broken off; and thou standest by faith." The Jews were cut off on account of their unbelief: we were grafted in on account of our belief. So notice: We live by faith, and we stand by faith.

Next: We walk by faith. Second Corinthians, chapter five, verse seven: "For we walk by faith, not by sight." The most faulty Christians I know are those who want to walk by sight.

They want to see the end — how a thing is going to come out. That isn't walking by faith at all — that is walking by sight.

I think the characters that best represent this difference are Joseph and Jacob. Jacob was a man who walked with God by sight. You remember his vow at Bethel: — "If God will be with me, and will keep me in this way that I go, and will give me bread to eat, and raiment to put on, so that I come again to my father's house in peace; then shall the Lord be my God." And you remember how his heart revived when he saw the wagons Joseph sent him from Egypt. He sought after signs. He never could have gone through the temptations and trials that his son Joseph did. Joseph represents a higher type of Christian. He could walk in the dark. He could survive thirteen years of misfortune, in spite of his dreams, and then ascribe it all to the goodness and providence of God.

Lot and Abraham are a good illustration. Lot turned away from Abraham and tented on the plains of Sodom. He got a good stretch of pasture land, but he had bad neighbors. He was a weak character and he should have kept with Abraham in order to get strong. A good many men are just like that. As long as their mothers are living, or they are bolstered up by some godly person, they get along very well; but they can't stand alone. Lot walked by sight; Abraham walked by faith; he went out in the footsteps of God. "By faith Abraham, when he was called to go out into a place which he should after receive for an inheritance, obeyed; and he went out, not knowing whither he went. By faith he sojourned in the land of promise, as in a strange country, dwelling in tabernacles with Isaac and Jacob, the heirs with him of the same promise: for he looked for a city which hath foundations, whose builder and maker is God." And again: We fight by faith. Ephesians, sixth chapter, verse sixteen: "Above all, taking the shield of faith, wherewith ye shall be able to quench all the fiery darts of the wicked." Every dart Satan can fire at us we can quench by faith. By faith we can overcome the Evil One. To fear is to have more faith in your antagonist than in Christ.

Some of the older people can remember when our war broke out. Secretary Seward, who was Lincoln's Secretary of State — a long-headed and shrewd politician — prophesied that the war would be over in ninety days; and young men in thousands and hundreds of thousands came forward and volunteered to go down to Dixie and whip the South. They thought they would be back in ninety days; but the war lasted four years, and cost about half a million of lives. What was the matter? Why, the South was a good deal stronger than the North supposed. Its strength was underestimated.

Jesus Christ makes no mistake of that kind. When He enlists a man in His service, He shows him the dark side; He lets him know that he must live a life of self-denial. If a man is not willing to go to heaven by the way of Calvary, he cannot go at all. Many men want a religion in which there is no cross, but they cannot enter heaven that way. If we are to be disciples of Jesus Christ, we must deny ourselves and take up our cross and follow Him. So let us sit down and count the cost. Do not think that you will have no battles if you follow the Nazarene, because many battles are before you. Yet if I had ten thousand lives, Jesus Christ should have every one of them. Men do not object to a battle if they are confident that they will have victory, and, thank God, every one of us may have the victory if we will.

The reason why so many Christians fail all through life is just this — they underestimate the strength of the enemy. My dear friend, you and I have got a terrible enemy to contend with. Don't let Satan deceive you. Unless you are spiritually dead, it means warfare. Nearly everything around tends to draw us away from God. We do not step clear out of Egypt on to the throne of God. There is the wilderness journey, and there are enemies in the land.

Don't let any man or woman think all he or she has to do is to join the church. That will not save you. The question is, are you overcoming the world, or is the world overcoming you? Are you more patient than you were five years ago? Are you more amiable? If you are not, the world is overcoming you, even if you are a church member. That epistle that Paul wrote to Titus says that we are to be sound in patience, faith and charity. We have got Christians, a good many of them, that are good in spots, but mighty poor in other spots. Just a little bit of them seems to be saved, you know. They are not rounded out in their characters. It is just because they haven't been taught that they have a terrible foe to overcome.

If I wanted to find out whether a man was a Christian, I wouldn't go to his minister. I would go and ask his wife. I tell you, we want more *home piety* just now. If a man doesn't treat his wife right, I don't want to hear him talk about Christianity. What is the use of his talking about salvation for the next life, if he has no salvation for this? We want a Christianity that goes into our homes and every day lives. Some men's religion just repels me. They put on a whining voice and a sort of a religious tone, and talk so sanctimoniously on Sunday that you would think they were wonderful saints. But on Monday they are quite different. They put their religion away with their clothes, and you don't see any more of it until the next Sunday. You laugh, but let us look out that we don't belong to that class. My friend, we have got to have a higher type of Christianity, or the Church is gone. It is wrong for a man or woman to profess what they don't possess. If you are not overcoming temptations, the world is overcoming you. Just get on your knees and ask God to help you. My dear friends, let us go to God and ask Him to search us. Let us ask Him to wake us up, and let us not think that just because we are church members we are all right. We are all wrong if we are not getting victory over sin.

TAKE YE AWAY THE STONE

IN THE gospel by John we read that at the tomb of Lazarus our Lord said to His disciples, "Take ye away the stone." Before the act of raising Lazarus could be performed, the disciples had their part to do. Christ could have removed the stone with a word. It would have been very easy for Him to have commanded it to roll away, and it would have obeyed His voice, as the dead Lazarus did when He called him back to life. But the Lord would have His children learn this lesson: that they have something to do towards raising the spiritually dead. The disciples had not only to take away the stone, but after Christ had raised Lazarus they had to "loose and let him go."

It is a question if any man on the face of the earth has ever been converted, without God using some human instument, in some way. God could easily convert men without us; but that is not His way.

The stone I want to speak about to-day, that must be rolled away before any great work of God can be brought about, is the miserable stone of prejudice. Many people have a great prejudice against revivals; they hate the very word. I am sorry to say that this feeling is not confined to ungodly or careless people; there are not a few Christians who seem to cherish a strong dislike both to the word "Revival" and to the thing itself.

What does "Revival" mean? It simply means a recalling from obscurity — a finding some hidden treasure and bringing it back to the light. I think every one of us must acknowledge that we are living in a time of need. I doubt if there is a family in the world that has not some relative whom they would like to see brought into the fold of God, and who needs salvation.

Men are anxious for a revival in business. I am told that there is a widespread and general stagnation in business. People are very anxious that there should be a revival of trade this winter. There is a great revival in politics just now. In all departments of life you find that men are very anxious for a revival in the things that concern them most.

If this is legitimate — and I do not say but it is perfectly right in its place — should not every child of God be praying for and desiring a revival of godliness in the world at the present time. Do we not need a revival of downright honesty, of truthfulness, of uprightness, and of temperance? Are there not many who have become alienated from the Church of God and from the house of the Lord, who are forming an attachment to the saloon? Are not our sons being drawn away by hundreds and thousands, so that while you often find the churches empty, the liquor shops are crowded every Sabbath afternoon and evening. I am sure the saloon-keepers are glad if they can have a revival in their business; they do not object to sell more whisky and beer. Then surely every true Christian ought to desire that men who are in danger of perishing eternally should be saved and rescued.

Some people seem to think that "Revivals" are a modern invention — that they have only been known within the last few years. But they are nothing new. If there is not Scriptural authority for revivals, then I cannot understand my Bible.

For the first 2,000 years of the world's history they had no revival that we know of; probably, if they had, there would have been no Flood. The first awakening, of which we read in the Old Testament, was when Moses was sent down to Egypt to bring his brethren out of the house of bondage. When Moses went down to Goshen, there must have been a great commotion there; many things were done out of the usual order. When three millions of Hebrews were put behind the Blood of the Slain Lamb, that was nothing but God reviving His work among them.

Under Joshua there was a great revival; and again under the Judges. God was constantly reviving the Jewish nation in those olden times. Samuel brought the people to Mizpah, and told them to put away their strange gods. Then the Israelites went out and defeated the Philistines, so that they never came back in his day. Dr. Bonar says it may be that David and Jonathan were converted under that revival in the time of Samuel.

What was it but a great revival in the days of Elijah? The people had turned away to idolatry, and the prophet summoned them to Mount Carmel. As the multitude stood there on the mountain, God answered by fire; the people fell on their faces and cried, "The Lord, He is the God." That was the nation turning back to God. No doubt there were men talking against the work, and saying it would not last. That is the cry of many to-day, and has been the cry for 4,000 years. Some old Carmelite very probably said in the days of Elijah: "This will not be permanent." So there are not a few in these days shaking their wise heads and saying the work will not last.

When we come to New Testament times, we have the wonderful revival under John the Baptist. Was there ever a man who accomplished so much in a few months, except the Master Himself? The preaching of John was like the breath of spring after a long and dreary winter. For 400 long years there had been no prophet, and darkness had settled down on the nation. John's advent was like the flashing of a brilliant meteor that heralded the coming day. It was not in the temple or in any synagogue that he preached, but on the banks of the Jordan. Men, women, and children flocked to hear him. Almost any one can get an audience in a crowded city, but this was away out in the desert. No doubt there was great excitement. I suppose the towns and villages were nearly depopulated, as they flocked out to hear the preaching of John.

People are so afraid of excitement. When I went over to England in 1867, I was asked to go and preach at the Derby race-course. I saw more excitement there in one day than I have seen at all the religious meetings I ever attended in my life put together. And yet I heard no one complaining of too much excitement. I heard of a minister, not long ago, who was present at a public dance till after five o'clock in the morning. The next Sabbath he preached against the excitement of revivals — the late hours, and so on. Very consistent kind of reasoning, was it not?

Then look at Pentecost. The apostles preached, and you know what the result was. I suppose the worldly men of that day said it would all die away. Although they brought about the martyrdom of Stephen and of James, other men rose up to take possession of the field. From the very place where Stephen was slain, Saul took up the work, and it has been going on ever since.

There are many professed Christians who are all the time finding fault and criticising. They criticise the preaching, or the singing. The prayers will be either too long or too short, too loud, or not loud enough. They will find fault with the reading of the Word of God, or will say it was not the right portion. They will criticise the preacher. "I do not like his style," they say. If you doubt what I say, listen to the people as they go out of a revival meeting, or any other religious gathering.

"What did you think of the preacher?" says one. "Well, I must confess I was disappointed. I did not like his manner. He was not graceful in his actions." Another will say: "He was not logical; I like logic." Or another: "He did not preach enough about repentance." If a preacher does not go over every doctrine in every sermon people begin to find fault. They say: "There was too much repentance, and no Gospel; or, it was all Gospel, and no repentance." "He spoke a great deal about justification, but he said nothing about sanctification." So if a man does not go right through the Bible, from Genesis to Revelation, in one sermon, they at once proceed to critise and find fault.

"The fact is," says some one of this class, "the man did not touch my heart at all." Some one else will say, "He was all heart and no head. I like a man to preach to my intellect." Or, "He appeals too much to the will; he does not give enough prominence to the doctrine of election." Or, again, "There is no backbone in his preaching; he does not lay sufficient stress on doctrine." Or, "He is not eloquent;" and so on, and so on.

You may find hundreds of such fault-finders among professed Christians; but all their criticism will not lead one solitary soul to Christ. I never preached a sermon yet that I could not pick to pieces and find fault with. I feel that Jesus Christ ought to have a far better representative than I am. But I have lived long enough to discover that there is nothing perfect in this world. If you are to wait until you can find a perfect preacher, or perfect meetings. I am afraid you will have to wait till the millennium arrives. What we want is to be looking right up to Him. Let us get done with fault-finding. When I hear people talk in the way I have described, I say to them, "Come and do better yourself. Step up here and try what you can do." My friends, it is so easy to find fault; it takes neither brains nor heart.

Some years ago, a pastor of a little Church in a small town became exceedingly discouraged, and brooded over his trials to such an extent that he became an inveterate grumbler. He found fault with his brethren because he imagined they did not treat him well. A brother minister was invited to assist him a few days in a special service. At the close of the Sabbath morning service our unhappy brother invited the minister to his house to dinner. While they were waiting alone in the parlor, he began his doleful story by saying: "My brother, you have no idea of my troubles; and one of the greatest is, my brethren in the Church treat me very badly." The other propounded the following questions:

"Did they ever spit in your face?"

"No; they haven't come to that."

"Did they ever smite you?" "No."

"Did they ever crown you with thorns?"

This last question he could not answer, but bowed his head thoughtfully. His brother replied: "Your Master and mine was thus treated, and all His disciples fled and left Him in the hands of the wicked. Yet He opened not His mouth." The effect of this conversation was wonderful. Both ministers bowed in prayer and earnestly sought to possess the mind which was in Christ Jesus. During the ten days' meetings the discontented pastor became *wonderfully changed*. He labored and prayed with his friend, and many souls were brought to Christ. Some weeks after, a deacon of the church wrote and said: "Your late visit and conversation with our pastor have had a wonderful influence for good. We never hear him complain now, and he labors more prayerfully and zealously." Another charge brought against revivals is that they are out of the regular order of things. Well, there is no doubt about that. But that does not prove that they are wrong. Eldad and Medad were out of the regular succession. Joshua wanted Moses to rebuke them. Instead of that he said: "Would God that all the Lord's people were prophets." Elijah and Elisha did not belong to the regular school of prophets, yet they exercised a mighty influence for good in their day. John the Baptist was not in the regular line. He got his theological training out in the desert. Jesus Christ Himself was out of the recognized order. When Philip told Nathaniel that he had found the Messiah, he said to him: "Can there any good thing come out of Nazareth?"

As we read the history of the past few centuries we find that God has frequently taken up those who were, so to speak, out of the regular line. Martin Luther had to break through the regular order of things in his day before he brought about the mighty Reformation. There are now some sixty millions of people who adhere to the Lutheran Church. Wesley and Whitefield were not exactly in the regular line, but see what a mighty work they accomplished!

My friends, when God works many things will be done "out of the regular order." It seems to me that will be a good thing. There are a few who cannot be reached, apparently, through the regular channels, who will come to meetings like these out of the usual routine. We have got our churches, it is true, but we want to make an effort to reach the outlying masses who will not go to them. Many will come in to these meetings simply because they are to be held only for a few days. And so, if they are to come at all, they must come to a decision about it quickly. Others come out of idle curiosity, or a desire to know what is going on. And often at the first meeting something that is spoken or that is sung will touch them. They have come under the sound of the Gospel; probably they will become real Christians and useful members of society. You will sometimes hear people say, "We have our churches; if men will not come to them, let them keep out." That was not the spirit of the Master. When our Civil War broke out we had a very small standing army. Government asked for volunteers to enlist. Several hundreds of thousands of men came forward and joined the ranks of the regular army. There was plenty for every man to do. These volunteers were not so well trained and drilled as the older soldiers, but we could use the irregulars as well as the regulars. Many of the former soon became efficient soldiers, and these volunteers did great service in the cause of the nation. If the outlying masses of the people are to be reached we must have the regulars and the irregulars both.

I remember hearing of a Sunday-school in our country where the teacher had got into ruts. A young man was placed in charge as Superintendent, and he wanted to re-arrange the seats. Some of the older members said the seats had been in their present position for so many years, that they could not be moved! There is a good deal of that kind of spirit nowadays. It seems to me that if one method is not successful we ought to give it up and try some other plan that may be more likely to succeed. If the people will not come to the regular "means of grace," let us adopt some means that will reach them and win them.

Do not let us be finding fault because things are not done exactly as they have been done in the past, and as we think they ought to be done. I am sick and tired of those who are constantly complaining. Let us pay no heed to them, but let us go forward with the work that God has given us to do.

Another very serious charge is brought against revivals. They say the work will not last. As I have said there were doubtless many at the day of Pentecost who said that. And when Stephen was stoned to death, James beheaded, and finally all the apostles put to death, no doubt they said that Pentecost was a stupendous failure. But was it a failure? Are not the fruits of that revival at Pentecost to be seen even in our time?

In the sight of the world the mission of John the Baptist may have been thought to be a failure when he was beheaded by the command of Herod. But it was not a failure in the sight of heaven. The influence of this wilderness prophet is felt in the Church of God to-day. The world thought Christ's life was a failure as He hung on the Cross and expired. But in the sight of God it was altogether different. God made the wrath of men to praise Him.

I have little sympathy with those pastors who, when God is reviving the Churches, begin to preach against revivals. There is not a denomination in Christendom to-day that has not sprung out of a revival. The Roman Catholics and the Episcopalians both claim to be apostolic in their origin; if they are, they sprang out of the revival at Pentecost. The Methodist body rose out of revivals under John Wesley and George Whitefield. Did not the

Lutheran Church come from the great awakening that swept through Germany in the days of Luther? Was not Scotland stirred up through the preaching of John Knox? Where did the Quakers come from if not from the work of God under George Fox? Yet people are so afraid if the regular routine of things is going to be disturbed. Let us pray that God may raise up many who will be used by Him for the reviving of His Church in our day. I think the time has come when we need it.

I remember we went into one place where one of the ministers found that his Church was opposed to his taking part in the meetings. He was told that if he identified himself with the movement he would alienate some of his congregation. He took the Church record and found that four-fifths of the members of the Church had been converted in times of revival, among others the Superintendent of the Sabbath-school, all the officers of the Church, and nearly every active member. The minister went into the Church the following Sabbath and preached a sermon on revivals, reminding them of what had taken place in the history of the congregation. You will find that many who talk against revivals have themselves been converted in such a time.

Not long ago a very able minister preached a sermon against these awakenings; he did not believe in them. Some of his people searched the Church records to see how many during the previous twelve years had been added to the membership on profession of their faith; they found that not a single soul had joined the Church all these years on profession of faith. No wonder the minister of a Church like that preached against revivals!

My experience has been that those who are converted in a time of special religious interest make even stronger Christians that those who were brought into the Church at ordinary times. One young convert helps another, and they get a better start in the Christian life when there are a good many together.

People say the converts will not hold out. Well, they did not all hold out under the preaching of Jesus Christ. "Many of His disciples went back and walked no more with Him." Paul mourned over the fact that some of those who made profession were walking as the enemies of the Cross of Christ. The Master taught in His wonderful parable that there are various kinds of hearers — those represented by the wayside hearers, the stony ground hearers, the thorny ground hearers, and the good ground hearers; they will remain to the end of time. I have a fruit tree at my home, and every year it has so many blossoms that if they should all produce apples the tree would break down. Nine tenths, perhaps, of the blossoms will fall off, and yet I have a large number of apples.

So there are many who make a profession of Christianity who fall away. It may be that those who seemed to promise the fairest turn out the worst, and those who did not promise so well turn out best in the end. God must prepare the ground and He must give the increase. I have often said that if I had to convict men of sin I would have given up the work long ago. That is the work of the Holy Ghost. What we have to do is to scatter the good seed of the Word, and expect that God will bless it to the saving of men's souls.

Of course we cannot expect much help from those who are all the time talking against revivals. I believe many young disciples are chilled through by those who condemn these special efforts. If the professed converts sometimes do not hold out, it is not always their own fault.

I was preaching in a certain city sometime ago, and a minister said to me: "I hope this work will not turn out like the revival here five years ago. I took one hundred converts into the Church, and, with the exception of one or two, I do not know where they are to-day." This was discouraging. I mentioned it to another minister in the same city, and I said I would rather give up the work, and go back to business, if the work was not going to last. He said to me: "I took in one hundred converts at the same time, and I can lay my hand hand on ninety-eight out of the hundred. For five years I have watched them, and only two have fallen away." Then he asked me if his brother minister had told me what took place in his Church after they brought in those young converts. Some of them thought they ought to have a better Church, and they got divided among themselves; so nearly all the members left the Church. If anyone will but engage heartily in this work they will have enough to encourage them.

It is very easy for men to talk against a work like this. But we generally find that such people not only do nothing at all themselves, but they know nothing about that which they are criticising. Surely it is hardly fair to condemn a work that we have not been at the trouble to become personally acquainted with. If, instead of sitting on the platform and simply looking on or criticising, such persons would get down among the people and talk to them about their souls, they would soon find out whether the work was real or not.

I remember hearing of a man who returned from a residence in India. He was out at dinner one day with some friends, and he was asked about Missions; he said he had never seen a native convert all the time he was in India. A missionary who was present did not reply directly to the statement, but he quietly asked the sceptical Englishman if he had seen any tigers in India. The man rubbed his hands, as if the recollection gave him a good deal of pleasure, and said: "Tigers! Yes, I should think so. I have shot a good many of them." Said the missionary, "Well, I was in India for a number of years and never saw a tiger." The fact was that the one had been looking for converts and the other for tigers, and they both found what they looked for.

If we look for converts we shall find them; there is no doubt about that. But the truth is that in almost every case those who talk against revivals know nothing whatever about it from personal contact and experience. Do you suppose that the young converts are going round to your house and knock at the door to tell you they have been converted? If you wish to find out the truth *you* must go among them in their homes and talk to them.

I hope no one will be afraid of the Inquiry Room. At one of the places where I worked once I found a good many people who hated the very word "Inquiry Room." But I contend that it is a perfectly reasonable thing. When a boy is at school and cannot solve some problem in algebra, he asks help of some one who knows it. Here is the great problem of eternal life that has to be solved by each of us. Why should we not ask those who are more experienced than ourselves to help us if they can. If we have any difficulty we cannot overcome, probably we shall find some Godly man or woman who had the same difficulty twenty years ago; they will be glad to help us, and tell us how they were enabled to surmount it. Do not be afraid therefore to let them help you.

I believe there is not a living soul who has a spiritual difficulty but there is some promise in the Word of God to meet that difficulty. But if you keep your feelings and your troubles all locked up, how are you to be helped? I might stand here and preach to you right on for thirty days and not touch your particular difficulty. But twenty minutes' private conversation may clear away all your doubts and troubles.

There was a lady who worked in the Inquiry Room when we were in the south of London nine years ago. I saw her again a short time ago, and she told me that she had a list of thirty-five cases of those with whom she conversed, and who she thought were truly converted. She has written letters to them and sent them little gifts at Christmas, and she said to me that so far as she could judge not a single one of the thirty-five had wandered away. She has placed her life alongside of theirs all these years, and she has been able to be a blessing to them.

If we had a thousand such persons, by the help of God we should see signs and wonders. There is no class of people, however hopeless or degraded, but can be reached, only we must lay ourselves out to reach them. Many Christians are asleep; we want to arouse them, so that they shall take a personal interest in those who are living in carelessness and sin. Let us lay aside all our prejudices. If God is working it matters little whether or not the work is done in the exact way that we would like to see it done, or in the way we have seen it done in the past.

Let there be one united cry going up to God, that He will revive His work in our midst. Let the work of revival begin with us who are Christians. Let us remove all the hindrances that come from ourselves. Then, by the help of the Spirit, we shall be able to reach these non-church goers, and multitudes will be brought into the kingdom of God.

THE PRAYERS OF THE BIBLE

THOSE WHO have left the deepest impression on this sin-cursed earth have been men and women of prayer. You will find that PRAYER has been the mighty power that has moved not only God, but man. Abraham was a man of prayer, and angels came down from heaven to converse with him. Jacob's prayer was answered in the wonderful interview at Peniel, that resulted in his having such a mighty blessing, and in softening the heart of his brother Esau; the child Samuel was given in answer to Hannah's prayer; Elijah's prayer closed up the heavens for three years and six months, and he prayed again and the heavens gave rain.

The Apostle James tells us that the prophet Elijah was a man "subject to like passions as we are." I am thankful that those men and women who were so mighty in prayer were just like ourselves. We are apt to think that those prophets and mighty men and women of old time were different from what we are. To be sure they lived in a much darker age, but they were of like passions with ourselves.

We read that on another occasion Elijah brought down fire on Mount Carmel. The prophets of Baal cried long and loud, but no answer came. The God of Elijah heard and answered his prayer. Let us remember that the God of Elijah still lives. The prophet was translated and went up to heaven, but his God still lives, and we have the same access to Him that Elijah had. We have the same warrant to go to God and ask the fire from

51

heaven to come down and consume our lusts and passions — to burn up our dross, and let Christ shine through us.

Elisha prayed, and life came back to a dead child. Many of our children are dead in trespasses and sins. Let us do as Elisha did; let us entreat God to raise them up in answer to our prayers.

Manasseh, the king, was a wicked man, and had done everything he could against the God of his father; yet in Babylon, when he cried to God, his cry was heard, and he was taken out of prison and put on the throne at Jerusalem. Surely if God gave heed to the prayer of wicked Manasseh, He will hear ours in the time of our distress. Is not this a time of distress with a great number of our fellow-men? Are there not many among us whose hearts are burdened? As we go to the throne of grace, let us remember that GOD ANSWERS PRAYER.

Look, again, at Samson. He prayed; and his strength came back, so that he slew more at his death than during his life. He was a restored backslider, and he had power with God. If those who have been backsliders will but return to God, they will see how quickly God will answer prayer.

Job prayed, and his captivity was turned. Light came in the place of darkness, and God lifted him up above the height of his former prosperity — in answer to prayer.

Daniel prayed to God, and Gabriel came to tell him that he was a man greatly beloved of God. Three times that message came to him from heaven in answer to prayer. The secrets of heaven were imparted to him, and he was told that God's Son was going to be cut off for the sins of His people. We find also that Cornelius prayed; and Peter was sent to tell him words whereby he and his should be saved. In answer to prayer this great blessing came upon him and his household. Peter had gone up to the house-top to pray in the afternoon, when he had that wonderful vision of the sheet let down from heaven. It was when prayer was made without ceasing unto God for Peter, that the angel was sent to deliver him.

So all through the Scriptures you will find that when believing prayer went up to God, the answer came down. I think it would be a very intresting study to go right through the Bible and see what has happened while God's people have been on their knees calling upon him. Certainly the study would greatly strengthen our faith — showing, as it would, how wonderfully God has heard and delivered, when the cry has gone up to Him for help.

Look at Paul and Silas in the prison at Philippi. As they prayed and sang praises, the place was shaken, and the jailor was converted. Probably that one conversion has done more than any other recorded in the Bible to bring people into the Kingdom of God. How many have been blessed in seeking to answer the question — "What must I do to be saved?" It was the prayer of those two godly men that brought the jailer to his knees, and that brought blessing to him and his family.

You remember how Stephen, as he prayed and looked up, saw the heavens opened, and the Son of Man at the right hand of God; the light of heaven fell on his face so that it shone. Remember, too, how the face of Moses shone as he came down from the Mount; he had been in communion with God. So when we get really into communion with God, He lifts up His countenance up on us; and instead of our having gloomy looks, our faces will shine, because God has heard and answered our prayers.

I want to call special attention to Christ as an example for us in all things; in nothing more than in prayer. We read that Christ prayed to His Father for everything. Every great crisis in His life was preceded by prayer. Let me quote a few passages. I never noticed till a few years ago that Christ was praying at His baptism. As He prayed, the heaven was opened, and the Holy Ghost descended on Him. Another great event in His life was His Transfiguration. "As He prayed, the fashion of His countenance was altered, and His raiment was white and glistening."

We read again: "It came to pass in those days that He went

out into a mountain to pray, and continued all night in prayer to God." This is the only place where it is recorded that the Savior spent a whole night in prayer. What was about to take place? When He came down from the mountain He gathered His disciples around Him, and preached that great discourse known as the Sermon on the Mount — the most wonderful sermon that has ever been preached to mortal men. Probably no sermon has done so much good, and it was preceded by a night of prayer. If our sermons are going to reach the hearts and consciences of the people, we must be much in prayer to God, that there may be power with the word.

In the Gospel of John we read that Jesus at the grave of Lazarus lifted up His eyes to heaven, and said: "Father, I thank Thee that Thou hast heard Me; and I know that Thou hearest Me always; but because of the people which stand by I said it, that they may believe that Thou hast sent Me." Notice, that before He spoke the dead to life He spoke to His Father. If our spiritually dead ones are to be raised, we must first get power with God. The reason we so often fail in moving our fellow-men is that we try to win them without first getting power with God. Jesus was in communion with His Father, and so He could be assured that His prayers were heard.

We read again, in the twelfth of John, that He prayed to the Father. I think this is one of the saddest chapters in the whole Bible. He was about to leave the Jewish nation and to make atonement for the sin of the world. Hear what He says: "Now is My soul troubled, and what shall I say? Father, save Me from this hour; but for this cause came I unto this hour." He was almost under the shadow of the Cross; the iniquities of mankind were about to be laid upon Him; one of His twelve disciples was going to deny Him and swear he never knew Him; another was to sell Him for thirty pieces of silver; all were to forsake Him and flee. His soul was exceeding sorrowful, and He prays; when His soul was troubled, God spake to Him.

Then in the Garden of Gethsemane, while He prayed, an angel appeared to strengthen him. In answer to His cry, "Father, glorify Thy Name," He hears a voice coming down from the glory — "I have both glorified it, and will glorify it again."

Another memorable prayer of our Lord was in the Garden of Gethsemane: "He was withdrawn from them about a stone's cast, and kneeled down and prayed." I would draw your attention to the recorded fact that four times the answer came right down from heaven while the Savior prayed to God. The first time was at His baptism, when the heavens were opened, and the Spirit descended upon Him in answer to His prayer. Again, on the Mount of Transfiguration, God appeared and spoke to Him. Then when the Greeks came desiring to see Him, the voice of God was heard responding to His call; and again, when He cried to the Father in the midst of His agony, a direct response was given. These things are recorded, I doubt not, that we may be encouraged to pray.

We read that His disciples came to Him, and said, "Lord, teach us to pray." It is not recorded that He taught them how to preach. I have often said that I would rather know how to pray like Daniel than to preach like Gabriel. If you get love into your soul, so that the grace of God may come down in answer to prayer, there will be no trouble about reaching the people. It is not by eloquent sermons that perishing souls are going to be reached; we need the power of God in order that the blessing may come down.

The prayer our Lord taught his disciples is commonly called the Lord's Prayer. I think that the Lord's prayer, more properly, is that in the seventeenth of John. That is the longest prayer on record that Jesus made. You can read it slowly and carefully in about four or five minutes. I think we may learn a lesson here. Our Master's prayers were short when offered in public; when He was alone with God that was a different thing, and He could spend the whole night in communion with His Father. My experience is that those who pray most in their closets generally make short prayers in public. Long prayers are too often not prayers at all, and they weary the people. How short the publican's prayer was: "God be merciful to me a sinner!" The Syrophenician woman's was shorter still: "Lord help me!" She went right to the mark, and she got what she wanted. The prayer of the thief on the cross was a short one: "Lord, remember me when Thou comest into Thy Kingdom!" Peter's prayer was, "Lord, save me, or I perish!" So, if you go through the Scriptures, you will find that the prayers that brought immediate answers were generally brief. Let our prayers be to the point, just telling God what we want.

In the prayer of our Lord, in John 17, we find that He made seven requests — one for Himself, four for His disciples around Him, and two for the disciples of succeeding ages. Six times in that one prayer He repeats that God had sent Him. The world looked upon Him as an imposter; and He wanted them to know that He was heaven-sent. He speaks of the world nine times, and makes mention of His disciples and those who believe on Him fifty times.

Christ's last prayer on the Cross was a short one: "Father, forgive them for they know not what they do." I believe that prayer was answered. We find that right there in front of the Cross, a Roman centurion was converted. It was probably in answer to the Savior's prayer. The conversion of the thief, I believe, was in answer to that prayer of our blessed Lord. Saul of Tarsus may have heard it, and the words may have followed him as he traveled to Damascus; so that when the Lord spoke to him on the way, he may have recognized the voice. One thing we do know; that on the day of Pentecost some of the enemies of the Lord were converted. Surely that was in answer to the prayer, "Father, forgive them!"

Hence we see that prayer holds a high place among the exercises of a spiritual life. All God's people have been praying people. Look, for instance, at Baxter! He stained his study walls with praying breath; and after he was anointed with the unction of the Holy Ghost, sent a river of living water over Kidderminster, and converted hundreds. Luther and his companions were men of such mighty pleading with God, that they broke the spell of ages, and laid nations subdued at the foot of the Cross. John Knox grasped all Scotland in his strong arms of faith, his prayers terrified tyrants. Whitefield, after much holy, faithful closet-pleading, went to the Devil's fair, and took more than a thousand souls out of the paw of the lion in one day. See a praying Wesley turn more than ten thousand souls to the Lord! Look at the praying Finney, whose prayers, faith, sermons and writings, have shaken this whole country, and sent a wave of blessing through the churches on both sides of the sea.

Dr. Guthrie thus speaks of prayer and its necessity: "The first true sign of spiritual life, prayer, is also the means of maintaining it. Man can as well live physically without breathing, as spiritually without praying. There is a class of animals — the cetaceous, neither fish nor sea-fowl — that inhabit the deep. It is their home, they never leave it for the shore; yet, though swimming beneath its waves, and sounding its darkest depths, they have ever and anon to rise to the surface that they may breathe the air. Without that, these monarchs of the deep could not exist in the dense element in which they live, and move, and have their being. And something like what is imposed on them by a physical necessity, the Christian has to do by a spiritual one. It is by ever and anon ascending up to God, by rising through prayer into a loftier, purer region for supplies of Divine grace, that he maintains his spiritual life. Prevent these animals from rising to the surface, and they die for want of breath; prevent the Christ from rising to God, and he dies for want of prayer. 'Give me children,' cried Rachel, 'or else I die.' 'Let me breathe,' says a man gasping, 'or else I die.' 'Let me pray,' says the Christian, 'or else I die.'"

"Since I began," said Dr. Payson when a student, "to beg God's blessing on my studies, I have done more in one week than in the whole year before." Luther, when most pressed with work, said, "I have so much to do that I cannot get on without three hours a day praying." And not only do theologians think and speak highly of prayer; men of all ranks and positions in life have felt the same. General Havelock rose at four o'clock, if the hour for marching was six, rather than lose the precious privilege of communion with God before setting out. Sir Matthew Hale says: "If I omit praying and reading God's Word in the morning, nothing goes well all day."

"A great part of my time," said McCheyne, "is spent in getting my heart in tune for prayer. It is the link that connects earth with heaven."

A comprehensive view of the subject will show that there are nine elements which are essential to true prayer. The first is Adoration; we cannot meet God on a level at the start. We must approach Him as One far beyond our reach or sight. The next is Confession; sin must be put out of the way. We cannot have any communion with God while there is any transgression between us. If there stands some wrong you have done a man, you cannot expect that man's favor until you go to him and confess the fault. Restitution is another; we have to make good the wrong, wherever possible. Thanksgiving is the next; we must be thankful for what God has done for us already. Then comes Forgiveness, and then Unity; and then for prayer, such as these things produce, there must be Faith. Thus influenced, we shall be ready to offer direct Petition. We hear a good deal of praying that is just exhorting, and if you did not see the man's eyes closed, you would suppose he was preaching. Then, much that is called prayer is simply finding fault. There needs to be more *petition* in our prayers. After all these, there must come Submission. While praying, we must be ready to accept the will of God. We shall consider these nine elements in detail, closing our inquiries by giving incidents illustrative of the certainty of our receiving, under such conditions, Answers to Prayer.

HEAVEN: ITS HOPE

*We give thanks to God and the Father of our Lord Jesus Christ
... for the* HOPE *which is laid up for you in heaven.*
— Colossians 1:3, 5

A GREAT MANY persons imagine that anything said about heaven
is only a matter of speculation. They talk about heaven much
as they would about the air. Now there would not have been
so much in Scripture on this subject if God had wanted to leave
the human race in darkness about it. "All Scripture," we are told,
"is given by inspiration of God, and is profitable for doctrine,
for reproof, for correction, for instruction in righteousness, that
the man of God may be perfect — thoroughly furnished unto all
good works" (II Tim. 3:16, 17). What the Bible says about heaven
is just as true as what it says about everything else. The Bible is
inspired. What we are taught about heaven could not have come
to us in any other way than by inspiration. No one knew anything
about it but God, and so if we want to find out anything about
it we have to turn to His Word. Dr. Hodge, of Princeton, says
that the best evidence of the Bible being the Word of God is
to be found between its own two covers. It proves itself. In this
respect it is like Christ, whose character proclaimed the divinity
of His person. Christ showed Himself more than man by what
He did. The Bible shows itself more than a human book by
what it says.

It is not, however, because the Bible is *written* with more
than human skill, far surpassing Shakespeare or any other human

author, and that its knowledge of character and the eloquence
it contains are beyond the powers of man, that we believe it to be
inspired. Men's ideas differ about the extent to which human
skill can be carried, but the reason why we believe the Bible to
be inspired is so simple that the humblest child of God can
comprehend it. If the proof of its divine origin lay in its wisdom
alone, a simple and uneducated man might not be able to believe
it. We believe it is inspired because there is nothing in it that
could *not* have come from God. God is wise, and God is good.
There is nothing in the Bible that is not wise, and there is
nothing in it that is not good. If the Bible had anything in it
that was opposed to reason, or to our sense of right, then, perhaps,
we might think that it was like all the books in the world that
are written merely by men. Books that are only human, like merely
human lives, have in them a great deal that is foolish and a
great deal that is wrong. The life of Christ alone was perfect,
being both human and divine. Not one of the other volumes,
like the Koran, that claims divinity of origin, agrees with common
sense. There is nothing at all in the Bible that does not conform
to common sense. What it tells us about the world having been
destroyed by a deluge, and Noah and his family alone being
saved, is no more wonderful than what is taught in the schools,
that all of the earth we see now, and everything upon it, came
out of a ball of fire. It is a great deal easier to believe that man
was made after the image of God, than to believe, as some young
men and women are being taught now, that he is the offspring
of a monkey.

Like all the other wonderful works of God, this Book bears
the sure stamp of its Author. It is like Him. Though man plants
the seeds, God makes the flowers, and they are perfect and
beautiful like Himself. Men wrote what is in the Bible, but the
work is God's. The more refined, as . a rule, people are, the
fonder they are of flowers, and the better they are, as a rule,
the more they love the Bible. The fondness for flowers refines

people, and the love of the Bible makes them better. All that is in the Bible about God, about man, about redemption, and about a future state, agrees with our own ideas of right, with our reasonable fears and with our personal experiences. All the historical events are described in the way that we know the world had of looking at them when they were written. What the Bible tells about heaven is not half so strange as what Prof. Proctor tells about the hosts of stars that are beyond the range of any ordinary telescope; and yet people very often think that science is all fact, and that religion is only fancy. A great many persons think that Jupiter and many more of the stars around us are inhabited, who cannot bring themselves to believe that there is beyond this earth a life for immortal souls. The true Christian puts faith before reason, and believes that reason always goes wrong when faith is set aside. If people would but read their Bibles more, and study what there is to be found there about heaven, they would not be as worldly-minded as they are. They would not have their hearts set upon things down here, but would seek the imperishable things above.

EARTH – THE HOME OF SIN

It seems perfectly reasonable that God should have given us a glimpse of the future, for we are constantly losing some of our friends by death, and the first thought that comes to us is, "Where have they gone?" When loved ones are taken away from us, how that thought comes up before us! How we wonder if we will ever see them again, and where and when it will be! Then it is that we turn to this blessed Book, for there is no other book in all the world that can give us the slightest comfort; no other book that can tell us where the loved ones have gone.

Not long ago I met an old friend, and as I took him by the hand and asked after his family, the tears came trickling down his cheeks as he said:

"I haven't any now."

"What," I said, "is your wife dead?"

"Yes, sir."

"And all your children, too?"

"Yes, all gone," he said, "and I am left here desolate and alone."

Would any one take from that man the hope that he will meet his dear ones again? Would any one persuade him that there is not a future where the lost will be found? No, we need not forget our dear loved ones; but we may cling forever to the enduring hope that there will be a time when we can meet unfettered, and be blest in that land of everlasting suns, where the soul drinks from the living streams of love that roll by God's high throne.

In our inmost hearts there are none of us but have questionings of the future.

> "Tell me, my secret soul,
>   O, tell me, Hope and Faith,
>   Is there no resting-place
>   From sorrow, sin and death?
>   Is there no happy spot
>   Where mortals may be blest,
>   Where grief may find a balm,
>   And weariness a rest?
> Faith, Hope and Love—best boons to mortals given—
> Waved their bright wings, and whispered:
>   Yes, in heaven!"

There are men who say that there is no heaven. I was once talking with a man who said he thought there was nothing to justify us in believing in any other heaven than that we know here on earth. If this is heaven, it is a very strange one—this world of sickness, sorrow and sin. I pity from the depths of my heart the man or woman who has that idea.

This world that some think is heaven, is the home of sin,

a hospital of sorrow, a place that has nothing in it to satisfy the soul. Men go all over it and then want to get out of it. The more men see of the world the less they think of it. People soon grow tired of the best pleasures it has to offer. Some one has said that the world is a stormy sea, whose every wave is strewed with the wrecks of mortals that perish in it. Every time we breathe some one is dying. We all know that we are going to stay here but a very little while. Our life is but a vapor. It is only a shadow.

"We meet one another," as some one has said, "salute one another, pass on and are gone." And another has said: "It is just an inch of time, and then eternal ages roll on"; and it seems to me that it is perfectly reasoable that we should study this Book, to find out where we are going, and where our friends are who have gone on before. The longest time man has to live has no more proportion to eternity than a drop of dew has to the ocean.

CITIES OF THE PAST

Look at the cities of the past. There is Babylon. It is said to have been founded by a queen named Semiramis, who had two millions of men at work for years building it. It is nothing but dust now. Nearly a thousand years ago, a historian wrote that the ruins of Nebuchadnezzar's palace were still standing, but men were afraid to go near them because they were full of scorpions and snakes. That is the sort of ruin that greatness often comes to in our own day. Nineveh is gone. Its towers and bastions have fallen. The traveler who tries to see Carthage cannot find much of it. Corinth, once the seat of luxury and art, is only a shapeless mass. Ephesus, long the metropolis of Asia, the Paris of that day, was crowded with buildings as large as the capitol at Washington. I am told it looks more like a neglected graveyard now than anything else. Granada, once so grand, with its twelve gates and towers, is now in decay. The Alhambra, the palace of the Mohammedan kings, was situated there. Little pieces of the once grand and beautiful cities of Herculanaeum and Pompeii are now being sold in the shops for relics. Jerusalem, once the joy of the whole earth, is but a shadow of its former self. Thebes, for thousands of years, up almost to the coming of Christ, among the largest and wealthiest cities of the world, is now a mass of decay. But little of ancient Athens, and many more of the proud cities of olden times, remain to tell the story of their downfall. God drives his plowshare through cities, and they are upheaved like furrows in the field. "Behold," says Isaiah, "the nations are as a drop of a bucket, and are counted as the small dust of the balance; behold, He taketh up the isles as a very little thing.... All nations before Him are as nothing; and they are counted to Him less than nothing, and vanity."

See how Antioch has fallen. When Paul preached there, it was a superb metropolis. A wide street, over three miles long, stretching across the entire city, was ornamented with rows of columns and covered galleries, and at every corner stood carved statues to commemorate their great men, whose names even we have never heard. These men are never heard of now, but the poor preaching tent-maker who entered its portals stands out as the grandest character in history. The finest specimens of Grecian art decorated the shrines of the temples, and the baths and the aqueducts were such as are never approached in elegance now. Men then, as now, were seeking honor, wealth and renown, and enshrining their names and records in perishable clay. Within the walls of Antioch, we are told, were enclosed hills, over seven hundred feet high, and rocky precipices and deep ravines gave a wild and picturesque character to the place of which no modern city affords an example. These heights were fortified in a marvelous manner, which gave to them strange and startling effects. The vast population of this brilliant city, combining all the art and cultivation of Greece with the levity, the luxury and the superstition of Asia, was as intent on pleasure as the population of any of our great cities are today. The citizens had their shows, their games, their races and dancers, their sorcerers, puzzlers, buffoons and miracle-workers, and the people sought constantly in the theaters and processions for something to stimulate and gratify the most corrupt desires of human nature. This is pretty much what we find the masses of the people in our great cities doing now.

Antioch was even worse than Athens, for the so-called worship they indulged in was not only idolatrous, but had mixed up with it the grossest passions to which man descends. It was here that Paul came to preach the glad tidings of the Gospel of Christ; it was here that the disciples were first called Christians, as a nickname; all followers of Christ before that time having been called "saints" or "brethren." As has been well said, out of that spring at Antioch a mighty stream has flowed to water the world. Astarte, the "Queen of Heaven," whom they worshiped; Diana, Apollo, the Pharisee and Sadducee, are no more, but the despised Christians yet live. Yet that heathen city, which would not take Christianity to its heart and keep it, fell. Cities that have not the refining and restraining influences of Christianity well established in them, seldom do amount to much in the long run. They grow dim in the light of ages. Few of our great cities in this country are a hundred years old as yet. For nearly a thousand years this city prospered; yet it fell.

GOING TO EMIGRATE

I do not think that it is wrong for us to think and talk about heaven. I'd like to locate heaven, and find out all I can about it. I expect to live there through all eternity. If I were going to dwell in any place in this country, if I were going to make it my home, I would want to inquire about the place, about its climate, about the neighbors I would have, about everything, in fact, that I could learn concerning it. If any of you were going to emigrate, that would be the way you would feel. Well, we are all going to emigrate in a very little while to a country that is very far away. We are going to spend eternity in another world, a grand and glorious world where God reigns. Is it not natural, then, that we should look and listen and try to find out who is already there, and what is the route to take?

Soon after I was converted, an infidel asked me one day why I looked *up* when I prayed. He said that heaven was no more above us than below us; that heaven was everywhere. Well, I was greatly bewildered, and the next time I prayed, it seemed almost as if I was praying into the air. Since then I have become better acquainted with the Bible, and I have come to see that heaven is above us; that it is upward, and not downward. The Spirit of God is everywhere, but God is in heaven, and heaven is above our heads. It does not matter what part of the globe we may stand upon, heaven is above us.

In the 17th chapter of Genesis it says that God went *up* from Abraham; and in the 3d chapter of John, that the Son of Man came *down* from heaven. So, in the 1st chapter of Acts we find that Christ went up into heaven (not down), and a cloud received him out of sight. Thus we see heaven is up. The very arrangement of the firmament about the earth declares the seat of God's glory to be above us. Job says: "Let not God regard it from *above*." Again, in Deuteronomy, we find, "who shall go *up* for us to heaven?" Thus, all through Scripture we find that we are given the location of heaven as upward and beyond the firmament. This firmament, with its many bright worlds scattered through, is so vast that heaven must be an extensive realm. Yet this need not surprise us. It is not for short-sighted man to inquire why God made heaven so extensive that its lights along the way can be seen from any part or side of this little world.

In Jeremiah 51:15, we are told: "He hath made the earth by His power; He hath established the world by His wisdom, and hath stretched out the heaven by His understanding." Yet, how little we really know of that power, or wisdom or understanding! As we read in Job: "Lo, these are parts of his ways; but how little a portion is heard of Him? But the thunder of His power, who can understand?"

This is the word of God. As we find in the 42nd chapter of Isaiah: "Thus saith God the Lord, He that created the heavens and stretched them out; He that spread forth the earth, and that which cometh out of it; He that giveth bread unto the people upon it, and spirit to them that walk within."

The discernment of God's power, the messages of heaven, do not always come in great things. We read in the 19th chapter of the first book of Kings:

"And, behold, the Lord passed by, and a great and strong wind rent the mountains, and brake pieces in the rocks before the Lord; but the Lord was not in the wind; and after the wind an earthquake; but the Lord was not in the earthquake; and after the earthquake a fire; but the Lord was not in the fire; and after the fire a still small voice."

It is as a still small voice that God speaks to His children. Some people are trying to find out just how far heaven is away. There is one thing we know about it; that is, that it is not so far away but that God can hear us when we pray. I do not believe there has ever been a tear shed for sin since Adam's fall in Eden to the present time, but God has witnessed it. He is not too far from earth for us to go to Him; and if there is a sigh that comes from a burdened heart today, God will hear that sigh. If there is a cry coming up from a heart broken on account of sin, God will hear that cry. He is not so far away, heaven is not so far away, as to be inaccessible to the smallest child. In II Chronicles we read:

"If My people, which are called by My name, shall humble themselves, and pray, and seek My face, and turn from their wicked ways, then will I hear from heaven, and will forgive them their sins, and will heal their land."

When I was in Dublin, they were telling me about a father who had lost a little boy. This father had not thought about the future, he had been so entirely taken up with this world and its affairs; but when that little boy, his only child, died, that father's heart was broken, and every night when he returned from work he might be found in his room with his candle and his Bible, hunting up all that he could find there about heaven. Some one asked him what he was doing, and he said he was trying to find out where his child had gone, and I think he was a reasonable man. I suppose no one will ever read this page who has not dear ones that are gone. Shall we close this Book today, or shall we look into it to try to find where the loved ones are? I was reading, some time ago, an account of a father, a minister, who had lost a child. He had gone to a great many funerals, offering comfort to others in sorrow, but now the iron had entered his own soul, and a brother minister had come to officiate and preach the funeral sermon; and after this minister had finished speaking, the father got up, and standing at the head of the coffin, he said that a few years ago, when he had first come into that parish, as he used to look over the river he took no interest in the people over there, because they were all strangers to him and there were none over there that had belonged to his parish. But, he said, a few years ago a young man came into his home, and married his daughter, and she went over the river to live, and when his child went over there, he became suddenly interested in the inhabitants, and every morning as he arose he would look out of the window across the river to her home. "But now," said he, "another child has been taken. She has gone over another river, and heaven seems dearer and nearer to me now than it ever has before."

My friends, let us believe this good old Book, be confident that heaven is not a myth, and be prepared to follow the dear ones who have gone before. Thus, and thus alone, can we find the peace we seek for.

SEEKING A BETTER COUNTRY

What has been, and is now, one of the strongest feelings in the human heart? Is it not to find some better place, some lovelier spot, than we have now? It is for this that men are seeking everywhere; and they can have it if they will; instead of looking down, they must look *up* to find it. As men grow in knowledge, they vie with each other more and more in making their homes attractive, but the brightest home on earth is but an empty barn, compared with the mansions in the skies.

What is it that we look for at the decline and close of life? Is it not some sheltered place, some quiet spot, where, if we cannot have constant rest, we may at least have a foretaste of the rest that is to be? What was it that led Columbus, not knowing what would be his fate, across the unsailed western seas, if it were not the hope of finding a better country? This it was that sustained the hearts of the Pilgrim Fathers, driven from their native land by persecution, as they faced an iron-bound, savage coast, with an unexplored territory beyond. They were cheered and upheld by the hope of reaching a free and fruitful country, where they could be at rest and worship God in peace.

Somewhat similar is the Christian's hope of heaven, only it is not an undiscovered country, and in attractions cannot be compared with anything we know on earth. Perhaps nothing but the shortness of our range of sight keeps us from seeing the celestial gates all open to us, and nothing but the deafness of our ears prevents our hearing the joyful ringing of the bells of heaven. There are constant sounds around us that we cannot hear, and the sky is studded with bright worlds that our eyes have never seen. Little as we know about this bright and radiant land, there are glimpses of its beauty that come to us now and then.

"We may not know how sweet its balmy air,
How bright and fair its flowers;
We may not hear the songs that echo there,
Through these enchanted bowers.

"The city's shining towers we may not see
With our dim earthly vision,
For Death, the silent warder, keeps the key
That opes the gates Elysian.

"But sometimes when adown the western sky
A fiery sunset lingers,
Its golden gate swings inward noiselessly,
Unlocked by unseen fingers.

"And while they stand a moment half ajar,
Gleams from the inner glory
Stream brightly through the azure vault afar,
And half reveal the story."

It is said by travelers that in climbing the Alps the houses of far distant villages can be seen with great distinctness, so that sometimes the number of panes of glass in a church window can be counted. The distance looks so short that the place to which the traveler is journeying appears almost at hand, but after hours and hours of climbing it seems no nearer yet. This is because of the clearness of the atmosphere. By perseverance, however, the place is reached at last, and the tired traveler finds rest. So sometimes we dwell in high altitudes of grace! heaven seems very near, and the hills of Beulah are in full view. At other times the clouds and fogs caused by suffering and sin cut off our sight. We are just as near heaven in the one case as we are in the other, and we are just as sure of gaining it if we only keep in the path that Christ has pointed out.

I have read that on the shores of the Adriatic sea the wives of fishermen, whose husbands have gone far out upon the deep, are in the habit of going down to the sea-shore at night and singing with their sweet voices the first verse of some beautiful hymn. After they have sung it they listen until they hear brought on the wind, across the sea, the second verse sung by their brave husbands as they are tossed by the gale— and both are happy. Perhaps, if we would listen, we too might hear on this storm-tossed world of ours, some sound, some whisper, borne from afar to tell us there is a Heaven which is our home; and when we sing our hymns upon the shores of the earth, perhaps we may hear their sweet echoes breaking in music upon the sands of time, and cheering the hearts of those who are pilgrims and strangers along the way. Yes, we need to look up—out, beyond this low earth, and to build higher in our thoughts and actions, even here!

You know, when a man is going up in a balloon, he takes in sand as ballast, and when he wants to mount a little higher, he throws out some of it, and then he will mount a little higher; he throws out a little more ballast, and he mounts still higher; and the more he throws out the higher he gets, and so the more we have to throw out of the things of this world the nearer we get to God. Let go of them; let us not set our hearts and affections on them, but do what the Master tells us—lay up for ourselves treasures in heaven.

In England I was told of a lady who had been bedridden for years. She was one of those saints whom God polishes up for the kingdom; for I believe there are many saints in this world whom we never hear about; we never see their names heralded through the press; they live very near the Master; they live very near heaven; and I think it takes a great deal more grace to suffer God's will than it does to do it; and if a person lies on a bed of sickness, and suffers cheerfully, it is just as acceptable to God as if they went out and worked in His vineyard.

Now this lady was of those saints. She said that for a long time she used to have a great deal of pleasure in watching a bird that came to make its nest near her window. One year it came to make its nest, and it began to build so low down she was afraid something would happen to the young; and every day that she saw that bird busy at work making its nest, she kept saying, "O bird, build higher!" She could see that the bird was likely to come to grief and disappointment. At last the bird got its nest done, and laid its eggs and hatched its young; and every morning the lady looked out to see if the nest was there, and she saw the old bird bringing food for the little ones, and she took a great deal of pleasure looking at it. But one morning she awoke, looked out, and she saw nothing but feathers scattered all around, and she said: "Ah, the cat has got the old bird and all her young." It would have been a kindness to have torn that nest down. That is what God does for us very often—just snatches things away before it is too late. Now, I think that is what we want to say to professing Christians—if you build for time you will be disappointed. God says: Build up yonder. It is a good deal better to have life with Christ in God than anywhere else. I would rather have my life hid with Christ in God than be in Eden as Adam was. Adam might have remained in Paradise for 16,000 years, and then fallen, but if our life is hid in Christ, how safe!

WITNESSING IN POWER

The subject of witness-bearing in the power of the Holy Ghost is not sufficiently understood by the Church. Until we have more intelligence on this point we are laboring under great disadvantage. Now, if you will take your Bible and turn to the 15th chapter of John and the 26th verse, you will find these words: "But when the Comforter is come, whom I will send unto you from the Father, even the Spirit of Truth, which proceedeth from the Father, He shall testify of me; and ye also shall bear witness, because ye have been with me from the beginning." Here we find what the Spirit is going to do, or what Christ said He would do when He came; namely, that He should testify of Him. And if you will turn over to the second chapter of Acts you will find that when Peter stood up on the day of Pentecost, and testified of what Christ had done, the Holy Spirit came down and bore witness to that fact, and men were convicted by hundreds and by thousands. So then man can not preach effectively of himself. He must have the Spirit of God to give ability, and study God's Word in order to testify according to the mind of the Spirit.

WHAT IS THE TESTIMONY?

If we keep back the Gospel of Christ and do not bring Christ before the people, then the Spirit has not the opportunity to work. But the moment Peter stood up on the day of Pentecost and bore testimony to this one fact, that Christ died for sin, and that He had been raised again, and ascended into heaven—the Spirit came down to bear witness to the Person and Work of Christ.

He came down to bear witness to the fact that Christ was in heaven, and if it was not for the Holy Ghost bearing witness to the preaching of the facts of the Gospel, do you think that the Church would have lived during these last eighteen centuries? Do you believe that Christ's death, resurrection and ascension would not have been forgotten as soon as His birth, if it had not been for the fact that the Holy Spirit had come? Because it is very clear, that when John made his appearance on the borders of the wilderness, they had forgotten all about the birth of Jesus Christ. Just thirty short years. It was all gone. They had forgotten the story of the Shepherds; they had forgotten the wonderful scene that took place in the temple, when the Son of God was brought into the temple and the older prophets and prophetesses were there; they had forgotten about the wise men coming to Jerusalem to inquire where He was that was born King of the Jews. That story of His birth seemed to have just faded away; they had forgotten all about it, and when John made his appearance on the borders of the wilderness it was brought back to their minds. And if it had not been for the Holy Ghost coming down to bear witness to Christ, to testify of His death and resurrection, these facts would have been forgotten as soon as His birth.

GREATER WORK

The witness of the Spirit is the witness of power. Jesus said, "The works that I do shall ye do also, and greater works than these shall ye do because I go to the Father." I used to stumble over that. I didn't understand it. I thought, what greater work could any man do than Christ had done? How could any one raise a dead man who had been laid away in the sepulcher for days, and who had already begun to turn back to dust; how with a word could he call him forth? But the longer I live the more

I am convinced it is a greater thing to influence a man's will; a man whose will is set against God; to have that will broken and brought into subjection to God's will—or, in other words, it is a greater thing to have power over a living, sinning, God-hating man, than to quicken the dead. He who could create a world could speak a dead soul into life; but I think the greatest miracle this world has ever seen was the miracle at Pentecost. Here were men who surrounded the Apostles, full of prejudice, full of malice, full of bitterness, their hands, as it were, dripping with the blood of the Son of God, and yet an unlettered man, a man whom they detested, a man whom they hated, stands up there and preaches the Gospel, and three thousand of them are immediately convicted and converted, and become disciples of the Lord Jesus Christ, and are willing to lay down their lives for the Son of God. It may have been on that occasion that Stephen was converted, the first martyr, and some of the men who soon after gave up their lives for Christ. This seems to me the greatest miracle this world has ever seen. But Peter did not labor alone; the Spirit of God was with him; hence the marvelous results.

The Jewish law required that there should be two witnesses, and so we find that when Peter preached there was a second witness. Peter testified of Christ, and Christ says when the Holy Spirit comes He will testify of Me. And they both bore witness to the verities of our Lord's incarnation, ministry, death, and resurrection, and the result was that a multitude turned as with one heart unto the Lord. Our failure now is, that preachers ignore the Cross, and veil Christ with sapless sermons and superfine language. They don't just present Him to the people plainly, and that is why, I believe, that the Spirit of God don't work with power in our churches. What we need is to preach Christ and present Him to a perishing world. The world can get on very well without you and me, but the world can not get on without Christ, and therefore we must testify of Him, and the world, I believe, today is just hungering and thirsting for this divine, satisfying portion. Thousands and thousands are sitting in darkness, knowing not of this great Light, but when we begin to preach Christ honestly, faithfully, sincerely and truthfully; holding Him up, not ourselves; exalting Christ and not our theories; presenting Christ and not our opinions; advocating Christ and not some false doctrine; then the Holy Ghost will come and bear witness. He will testify that what we say is true. When He comes He will confirm the Word with signs following. This is one of the strongest proofs that our Gospel's Divine; that it is of Divine origin; that not only did Christ teach these things, but when leaving the world He said, "He shall glorify Me," and "He will testify of Me." If you will just look at the second chapter of Acts—to that wonderful sermon that Peter preached—the thirty-sixth verse, you read these words: "Therefore let all the house of Israel know assuredly that God hath made that same Jesus whom ye crucified, both Lord and Christ." And when Peter said this the Holy Ghost descended upon the people and testified of Christ—bore witness in signal demonstration that all this was true. And again, in the fortieth verse, "And with many other words did He testify and exhort, saying, Save yourselves from this untoward generation." With many other words did He testify, not only these words that have been recorded, but many other words.

THE SURE GUIDE

Turn to the sixteenth chapter of John, in the thirteenth verse, and read: "Howbeit, when He, the Spirit of Truth is come, He will guide you into all truth; for He shall not speak of Himself; but whatsoever He shall hear that shall He speak; and He will show you things to come." He will guide you into all truth. Now there is not a truth that we ought to know but the Spirit of God will guide us into it if we will let Him; if we will yield ourselves up to be directed by the Spirit, and let

Him lead us, He will guide us into all truth. It would have saved us from a great many dark hours if we had only been willing to let the Spirit of God be our counsellor and guide.

Lot never would have gone to Sodom if he had been guided by the Spirit of God. David never would have fallen into sin and had all that trouble with his family if he had been guided by the Spirit of God.

There are many Lots and Davids now-a-day. The churches are full of them. Men and women are in total darkness, because they have not been willing to be guided by the Spirit of God. "He shall guide you into all truth. He shall not speak of Himself." He shall speak of the ascended glorified Christ.

What would be thought of a messenger, entrusted by an absent husband with a message for his wife or mother who, on arrival, only talked of himself, and his conceits, and ignored both the husband and the message? You would simply call it outrageous. What then must be the crime of the professed teacher who speaks of himself, or some insipid theory, leaving out Christ and His Gospel? If we witness according to the Spirit, we must witness of Jesus.

The Holy Spirit is down here in this dark world to just speak of the Absent One, and He takes the things of Christ and brings them to our mind. He testifies of Christ; He guides us into the the truth about Him.

RAPPINGS IN THE DARK

I want to say right here, that I think in this day a great many children of God are turning aside and committing a grievous sin. I don't know as they think it is a sin, but if we examine the Scriptures, I am sure we will find that it is a great sin. We are told that the Comforter is sent into the world to "guide us into all truth," and if He is sent for that purpose, do we need any other guide? Need we hide in the darkness, consulting with mediums, who profess to call up the spirits of the dead? Do you know what the Word of God pronounces against that fearful sin? I believe it is one of the greatest sins we have to contend with at the present day. It is dishonoring to the Holy Spirit for me to go and summon up the dead and confer with them, even if it were possible.

I would like you to notice the 10th chapter of 1st Chronicles, and 13th verse: "So Saul died for his transgression which he had committed against the Lord, even against the Word of the Lord, which he kept not, and also for asking counsel of one that had a familiar spirit, to inquire of it; and inquired not of the Lord: therefore He slew him, and turned the kingdom unto David the son of Jesse."

God slew him for this very sin. Of the two sins that are brought against Saul here, one is that he would not listen to the Word of God, and the second is that he consulted a familiar spirit. He was snared by this great evil, and sinned against God.

Saul fell right here, and there are a great many of God's professed children to-day who think there is no harm in consulting a medium who pretends to call up some of the departed to inquire of them.

But how dishonoring it is to God who has sent the Holy Spirit into this world to guide us "into all truth." There is not a thing that I need to know, there is not a thing that is important for me to know; there is not a thing that I ought to know but the Spirit of God will reveal it to me through the Word of God, and if I turn my back upon the Holy Spirit, I am dishonoring the Spirit of God, and I am committing a grievous sin. You know we read in Luke, where that rich man in the other world wanted to have some one sent to his father's house to warn his five brothers, Christ said they have Moses and the prophets, and if they will not hear them, they will not hear one though he rose from the dead. Moses and the prophets, the part of the Bible then completed, that is enough. But a great many people now want something besides the Word of God, and are turning aside to these false lights.

SPIRITS THAT PEEP AND MUTTER

There is another passage which reads, "And when they shall say unto you, seek unto them that have familiar spirits, and unto wizards that peep and mutter: Should not a people seek unto their God? for the living to the dead?" What is that but table-rapping, and cabinet-hiding? If it was a message from God, do you think you would have to go into a dark room and put out all the lights? In secret my Master taught nothing. God is not in that movement, and what we want, as children of God, is to keep ourselves from this evil. And then notice the verse following, quoted so often out of its connection. "To the law and to the testimony; if they speak not according to this word, it is because there is no light in them." Any man, any woman, who comes to us with any doctrine that is not according to the law and the testimony, let us understand that they are from the evil one, and that they are enemies of righteousness. They have no light in them. Now you will find these people who are consulting familiar spirits, first and last, attack the Word of God. They don't believe it. Still a great many people say, you must hear both sides—but if a man should write me a most slanderous letter about my wife, I don't think I would have to read it; I should tear it up and throw it to the winds. Have I to read all the infidel books that are written, to hear both sides? Have I to take up a book that is a slander on my Lord and Master, who has redeemed me with His blood? Ten thousand times No; I will not touch it.

"Now the Spirit speaketh expressly, that in the latter times some shall depart from the faith, giving heed to seducing spirits, and the doctrines of devils (I Tim. 4:1). That is pretty plain language, isn't it? "Doctrines of devils." Again, "speaking lies in hypocrisy; having their consciences seared with a hot iron."

There are other passages of Scripture warning against every delusion of Satan. Let us ever remember the Spirit has been sent into the world to guide us into all truth. We don't want any other guide; He is enough. Some people say, "Is not conscience a safer guide than the Word and the Spirit?" No, it is not. Some people don't seem to have any conscience, and don't know what it means. Their education has a good deal to do with conscience. There are persons who will say that their conscience did not tell them that they had done wrong until after the wrong was done; but what we want, is something to tell us a thing is wrong before we do it. Very often a man will go and commit some awful crime, and after it is done his conscience will wake up and lash and scourge him, and then it is too late, the act is done.

THE UNERRING GUIDE

I am told by people who have been over the Alps, that the guide fastens them, if they are going in a dangerous place, right to himself, and he just goes on before; they are fastened to the guide.

And so should the Christian be linked to His unerring Guide, and be safely upheld. Why, if a man was going through the Mammoth Cave, it would be death to him if he strayed away from his guide—if separated from him, he would certainly perish; there are pitfalls in that cave and a bottomless river, and there would be no chance for a man to find his way through that cave without a guide or a light. So there is no chance for us to get through the dark wilderness of this world alone. It is folly for a man or woman to think that they can get through this evil world without the light of God's Word and the guidance of the Divine Spirit. God sent Him to guide us through this great journey, and if we seek to work independent of Him, we shall stumble into the deep darkness of eternity's night.

But bear in mind the *Words* of the Spirit of God; if you want to be guided, you must study the Word; because the Word is the light of the Spirit. In the 14th chapter of John and 26th verse, we read:

"But the Comforter, which is the Holy Ghost, whom the Father will send in my name, He shall teach you all things, and bring all things to your remembrance, whatsoever I have said unto you."

Again in John 16:13:

"Howbeit when He, the Spirit of Truth, is come, He will guide you into all truth: for He shall not speak of Himself; but whatsoever He shall hear, that shall He speak: and He will show you things to come."

"He will show you things to come." A great many people seem to think that the Bible is out of date, that it is an old book, and they think it has passed its day. They say it was very good for the dark ages, and that there is some very good history in it; but then it was not intended for the present time; that we are living in a very enlightened age, and that men can get on very well without the old book; that we have out-grown it. They think we have no use for it, because it is an old book. Now you might just as well say that the sun, which has shone so long, is now so old that it is out of date, and that whenever a man builds a house he need not put any windows in it, because we got a newer light and a better light; we have gaslight and this new electric light. These are something new; and I would advise people, if they think the Bible is too old and worn out, when they build houses, not to put any windows in them, but just to light them with this new electric light; that is something new, and this is what they are anxious for. People talk about this Book as if they understood it; but we don't know much about it yet. The press gives us the daily news of what has taken place. This Bible, however, tells us what is about to take place. This *is* new; we have the news here in this Book; this tells us of the things that will surely come to pass; and that is a great deal newer than anything in the newspapers. It tells us that the Spirit shall teach us all things; not only guide us into all truth, but teach us all things; He teaches us how to pray, and I don't think there has ever been a prayer upon this sin-cursed earth that has been indicted by the Holy Spirit but was answered. There is much praying that is not indicted by the Holy Spirit. In former years I was very ambitious to get rich; I used to pray for one hundred thousand dollars; that was my aim, and I used to say, "God does not answer my prayer; He does not make me rich." But I had no warrant for such a prayer; yet a good many people pray in that way; they think that they pray, but they do not pray according to the Scriptures. The Spirit of God has nothing to do with their prayers, and such prayers are not the product of His teaching.

It is the Spirit who teaches us how to answer our enemies. If a man strikes me, I should not pull out a revolver and shoot him. The Spirit of the Lord doesn't teach me revenge; He don't teach me that it is necessary to draw the sword and cut a man down in order to defend my rights. Some people say, You are a coward if you don't strike back. Christ says, turn the other cheek to him who smites. I would rather take Christ's teaching than any other. I don't think a man gains much by loading himself down with weapons to defend himself. There has been life enough sacrificed in this country to teach men a lesson in this regard. The Word of God is a much better protection than the revolver. We had better take the Word of God to protect us, by accepting its teaching, and living out its precepts.

AN AID TO MEMORY

It is a great comfort to us to remember that another office of the Spirit is to bring the teaching of Jesus to our remembrance. This was our Lord's promise, "He shall teach you all things, and brings all things to your remembrance" (John 14:26).

How striking that is. I think there are many Christians who

have had that experience. They have been testifying, and found that while talking for Christ the Spirit has just brought into mind some of the sayings of the Lord Jesus Christ, and their mind was soon filled with the Word of God. When we have the Spirit resting upon us, we can speak with authority and power, and the Lord will bless our testimony and bless our work. I believe the reason why God makes use of so few in the Church, is because there is not in them the power that God can use. He is not going to use our ideas, but we must have the Word of God hid in our hearts, and then, the Holy Spirit inflaming us, we will have the testimony which will be rich, and sweet, and fresh, and the Lord's Word will vindicate itself in blessed results. God wants to use us; God wants to make us channels of blessing; but we are in such a condition He does not use us. That is the trouble; there are so many men who have no testimony for the Lord; if they speak, they speak without saying anything, and if they pray, their prayer is powerless; they do not plead in prayer; their prayer is just a few set phrases that you have heard too often. Now what we want, is to be so full of the Word, that the Spirit coming upon us shall bring to mind — bring to our remembrance — the words of the Lord Jesus.

In I Corinthians 2:9 it is written: "Eye hath not seen, nor ear heard, neither have entered into the heart of man the things which God hath prepared for them that love Him."

We hear that quoted so often in prayer — many a man weaves it into his prayer and stops right there. And the moment you talk about Heaven, they say, "Oh, we don't know anything about Heaven; it hath not entered into the heart of man; eye hath not seen; it is all speculation; we have nothing to do with it"; and they say they quote it as it is written. "Eye hath not seen, nor ear heard; neither have entered into the heart of man the things which God hath prepared for them that love Him." What next — "but God hath revealed them unto us by His Spirit." You see the Lord hath revelaed them unto us: "For the

Spirit searches all things — yea, the deep things of God." That is just what the Spirit does.

LONG AND SHORT SIGHT

He brings to our mind what God has in store for us. I heard a man, some time ago, speaking about Abraham. He said "Abraham was not tempted by the well-watered plains of Sodom, for Abraham was what you might call a long-sighted man; he had his eyes set on the city which had foundation — 'whose Builder and Maker is God.'" But Lot was a short-sighted man; and there are many people in the Church who are very short-sighted; they only see things right around them they think good. Abraham was long-sighted; he had glimpses of the celestial city. Moses was long-sighted, and he left the palaces of Egypt and identified himself with God's people — poor people, who were slaves; but he had something in view yonder; he could see something God had in store. Again there are some people who are sort of long-sighted and short-sighted, too. I have a friend who has one eye that is long-sighted and the other is short-sighted; and I think the Church is full of this kind of people. They want one eye for the world and the other for the Kingdom of God. Therefore, everything is blurred, one eye is long and the other is short, all is confusion, and they "see men as trees walking." The Church is filled with that sort of people. But Stephen was long-sighted; he looked clear into heaven; they couldn't convince him even when he was dying, that Christ had not ascended to heaven. "Look yonder," he says, "I see Him over there; He is on the throne, standing at the right hand of God"; and he looked clear into heaven; the world had no temptation for him; he had put the world under his feet. Paul was another of those long-sighted men; he had been caught up and seen things unlawful for him to utter; things grand and glorious. I tell you when the Spirit of God is on us the world looks very empty; the world has a very small hold upon us, and we begin to let go our hold of it. When the Spirit of God is on us we will just let go the things of time and lay hold of things eternal. This is the Church's need to-day; we want the Spirit to come in mighty power, and consume all the vile dross there is in us. Oh! that the Spirit of fire may come down and burn everything in us that is contrary to God's blessed Word and Will.

In John 15:16, we read of the Comforter. This is the first time He is spoken of as the Comforter. Christ had been their Comforter. God had sent Him to comfort the sorrowing. It was prophesied of Him, "The Spirit of the Lord is upon me, because He hath anointed me to preach the Gospel to the poor; He has sent me to heal the broken-hearted." You can't heal the broken-hearted without the Comforter; but the world would not have the first Comforter, and so they rose up and took Him to Calvary and put him to death; but on going away He said, "I will send you another Comforter; you shall not be comfortless; be of good cheer, little flock; it is the Father's good pleasure to give you the kingdom." All these sweet passages are brought to the remembrance of God's people, and they help us to rise out of the fog and mist of this world. O, what a comforter is the Holy Spirit of God!

THE FAITHFUL FRIEND

The Holy Spirit tells a man of his faults in order to lead him to a better life. In John 16:8, we read: "He is to reprove the world of sin." Now, there are a class of people who don't like this part of the Spirit's work. Do you know why? Because He convicts *them* of sin; they don't like that. What they want is some one to speak comforting words and make everything pleasant; keep everything all quiet; tell them there is peace when there is war; tell them it is light when it is dark, and tell them everything is growing better; that the world is getting on amazingly in goodness; that it is growing better all the time; that is the kind of preaching they seek for. Men think they are a great deal better than their fathers were. That suits human nature, for it is full of pride. Men will strut around and say, "Yes, I believe that; the world is improving; I am a good deal better man than father was; my father was too strict; he was one of those old Puritanical men who was so rigid. O, we are getting on; we are more liberal; my father wouldn't think of going out riding on Sunday, but we will; we will trample the laws of God under our feet; we are better than our fathers."

That is the kind of preaching which some dearly love, and there are preachers who tickle such itching ears. When you bring the Word of God to bear upon them, and when the Spirit drives it home, then men will say: "I don't like that kind of preaching; I will never go to hear that man again;" and sometimes they will get up and stamp their way out of church before the speaker gets through; they don't like it. But when the Spirit of God is at work he convicts men of sin. "When He comes He will reprove the world of sin, of righteousness and of judgment; of sin" — not because men swear and lie and steal and get drunk and murder — "of sin because they believe not on Me."

THE CLIMAX SIN

That is the sin of the world. Why, a great many people think that unbelief is a sort of misfortune, but do not know, if you will allow me the expression, it is the damning sin of the world to-day; that is what unbelief is, the mother of all sin. There would not be a drunkard walking the streets, if it were not for unbelief; there would not be a harlot walking the streets, if it were not for unbelief; there would not be a murderer, if it was not for unbelief; it is the germ of all sin. Don't think for a moment that it is a misfortune, but just bear in mind it is an awful sin, and may the Holy Spirit convict every reader that unbelief is making God a liar. Many a man has been knocked down on the streets because some one has told him he was a liar. Unbelief is giving God the lie; that is the plain English of it. Some people seem to boast of their unbelief; they seem to think it is quite respectable to be an infidel and doubt God's Word, and they will vainly boast and say, "I have intellectual difficulties; I can't believe." Oh that the Spirit of God may come and convict men of sin! That is what we need — His convicting power, and I am so thankful that God has not put that into our hands. We have not to convict men; if we had I would get discouraged, and give up preaching and go back to business within the next forty-eight hours. It is my work to preach and hold up the Cross and testify of Christ; but it is His work to convict men of sin and lead them to Christ. One thing I have noticed, that some conversions don't amount to anything; that if a man professes to be converted without conviction of sin, he is one of those stony-ground hearers who don't bring forth much fruit. The first little wave of persecution, the first breath of opposition, and the man is back in the world again. Let us pray, dear Christian reader, that God may carry on a deep and thorough work, that men may be convicted of sin so that they can not rest in unbelief. Let us pray God it may be a thorough work in the land. I would a great deal rather see a hundred men thoroughly converted, truly born of God, than to see a thousand professed conversions where the Spirit of God has not convicted of sin. Don't let us cry "Peace, peace, when there is no peace." Don't go to the man who is living in sin, and tell him all he has to do is to stand right up and profess, without any hatred for sin. Let us ask God first to show every man the plague of his own heart, that the Spirit, may convict them of sin. Then will the work in our hands be real, and deep, and abide the fiery trial which will try every man's labor.

Thus far, we have found the work of the Spirit is to impart life, to implant hope, to give liberty, to testify of Christ, to guide us into all truth, to teach us all things, to comfort the believers, and to convict the world of sin.

"Holy Spirit, faithful guide,
Ever near the Christian's side;
Gently lead us by the hand,
Pilgrims in a desert land;
Weary souls for e'er rejoice,
While they hear that sweetest voice,
Whisp'ring softly, wanderer come!
Follow Me, I'll guide thee home.

"Ever present, truest Friend,
Ever near Thine aid to lend,
Leave us not to doubt and fear,
Groping on in darkness drear,
When the storms are raging sore,
Hearts grow faint, and hopes give o'er;
Whisp'ring softly, wanderer come!
Follow Me, I'll guide thee home.

"When our days of toil shall cease,
Waiting still for sweet release,
Nothing left but heaven and prayer,
Wond'ring if our names were there,
Wading deep the dismal flood,
Pleading nought but Jesus' blood;
Whisp'ring softly, wanderer come!
Follow Me, I'll guide thee home.

THE GATEWAY INTO THE KINGDOM

Except a man be born again he cannot enter the kingdom of God. — John 3:3

THERE IS no portion of the Word of God, perhaps, with which we are more familiar than this passage. I suppose if I were to ask those in any audience if they believed that Jesus Christ taught the doctrine of the New Birth, nine-tenths of them would say: "Yes, I believe He did."

Now if the words of this text are true they embody one of the most solemn questions that can come before us. We can afford to be deceived about many things rather than about this one thing. Christ makes it very plain. He says, "Except a man be born again, he cannot *see* the Kingdom of God" — much less inherit it. This doctrine of the New Birth is therefore the foundation of all our hopes for the world to come. It is really the A B C of the Christian religion. My experience has been this — that if a man is unsound on this doctrine he will be unsound on almost every other fundamental doctrine in the Bible. A true understanding of this subject will help a man to solve a thousand difficulties that he may meet with in the Word of God. Things that before seemed very dark and mysterious will become very plain.

The doctrine of the New Birth upsets all false religion — all false views about the Bible and about God. A friend of mine once told me that in one of his after-meetings, a man came to him with a long list of questions written out for him to answer.

He said: "If you can answer these questions satisfactorily, I have made up my mind to be a Christian." "Do you not think," said my friend, "that you had better come to Christ first? Then you can look into these questions." The man thought that perhaps he had better do so. After he had received Christ, he looked again at his list of questions; but then it seemed to him as if they had all been answered. Nicodemus came with his troubled mind, and Christ said to him, "Ye must be born again." He was treated altogether differently from what he expected; but I venture to say that was the most blessed night in all his life. To be "born again" is the greatest blessing that will ever come to us in this world.

Notice how the Scripture puts it. "Except a man be born again," "born from above," "born of the Spirit." From amongst a number of other passages where we find this word "EXCEPT," I would just name three. "Except ye repent, ye shall all likewise perish" (Luke 13:3, 5). "Except ye be converted, and become as little children, ye shall not enter into the kingdom of heaven" (Matt. 18:3). "Except your righteousness shall exceed the righteousness of the Scribes and Pharisees, ye shall in no case enter into the kingdom of heaven" (Matt. 5:20). They all really mean the same thing.

I am so thankful that our Lord spoke of the New Birth to this ruler of the Jews, this doctor of the law, rather than to the woman at the well of Samaria, or to Matthew the publican, or to Zaccheus. If He had reserved his teaching on this great matter for these three, or such as these, people would have said: "Oh yes, these publicans and harlots need to be converted: but I am an upright man; I do not need to be converted." I suppose Nicodemus was one of the best specimens of the people of Jerusalem: there was nothing on record against him.

I think it is scarcely necessary for me to prove that we need to be born again before we are meet for heaven. I venture to say that there is no candid man but would say he is not fit for the kingdom of God, until he is born of another Spirit. The Bible teaches us that man by nature is lost and guilty, and our experience confirms this. We know also that the best and holiest man, if he turn away from God, will very soon fall into sin.

Now, let me say what Regeneration is not. It is not going to church. Very often I see people, and ask them if they are Christians. "Yes, of course I am; at least, I think I am: I go to church every Sunday." Ah, but this is not Regeneration. Others say, "I am trying to do what is right — am I not a Christian? Is not that a new birth?" No. What has that to do with being born again? There is yet another class — those who have "turned over a new leaf," and think they are regenerated. No; forming a new resolution is not being born again.

Nor will being baptized do you any good. Yet you hear people say, "Why, I have been baptized; and I was born again when I was baptized." They believe that because they were baptized into the church, they were baptized into the Kingdom of God. I tell you that it is utterly impossible. You may be baptized into the church, and yet not be baptized into the Son of God. Baptism is all right in its place. God forbid that I should say anything against it. But if you put that in the place of Regeneration — in the place of the New Birth — it is a terrible mistake. You cannot be baptized into the Kingdom of God. "Except a man be BORN AGAIN, he cannot see the Kingdom of God." If any one reading this rests his hopes on anything else — on any other foundation — I pray that God may sweep it away.

Another class say, "I go to the Lord's Supper; I partake uniformly of the Sacrament." Blessed ordinance! Jesus hath said that as often as ye do it ye commemorate His death. Yet, that is not being "born again;" that is not passing from death unto life. Jesus says plainly — and so plainly that there need not be any mistake about it — "Except a man be born of the Spirit, he cannot enter into the Kingdom of God." What has a sacrament to do with that? What has going to church to do with being born again?

Another man comes up and says, "I say my prayers regularly." Still I say that is not being born of the Spirit. It is a very solemn question, then, that comes up before us; and oh! that every reader would ask himself earnestly and faithfully: "Have I been born again? Have I been born of the Spirit? Have I passed from death unto life?"

There is a class of men who say that special religious meetings are very good for a certain class of people. They would be very good if you could get the drunkard here, or get the gambler there, or get other vicious people there — that would do a great deal of good. But "we do not need to be converted." To whom did Christ utter these words of wisdom? To Nicodemus. Who was Nicodemus? Was he a drunkard, a gambler, or a thief? No! No doubt he was one of the very best men in Jerusalem. He was an honorable Councillor; he belonged to the Sanhedrim; he held a very high position; he was an orthodox man; he was one of the very soundest men. And yet what did Christ say to him? "Except a man be born again, he *cannot see* the kingdom of God."

But I can imagine some one saying, "What am I to do? I cannot create life. I certainly cannot save myself." You certainly cannot; and we do not claim that you can. We tell you it is utterly impossible to make a man better without Christ; but that is what men are trying to do. They are trying to patch up this "old Adam" nature. THERE MUST BE A NEW CREATION. Regeneration is a new creation; and if it is a new creation it must be the work of God. In the first chapter of Genesis man does not appear. There is no one there but God. Man is not there to take part. When God created the earth He was alone. When Christ redeemed the world He was alone.

"That which is born of the flesh is flesh; and that which is born of the Spirit is spirit" (John 3:6). The Ethiopian cannot change his skin, and the leopard cannot change his spots. You might as well try to make yourselves pure and holy without the help of God. It would be just as easy for you to do that as for the black man to wash himself white. A man might just as well try to leap over the moon as to serve God in the flesh. Therefore, "that which is born of the flesh is flesh; and that which is born of the Spirit is spirit."

Now God tells us in this chapter how we are to get into His kingdom. We are not to work our way in — not but that salvation is worth working for. We admit all that. If there were rivers and mountains in the way, it would be well worth while to swim those rivers, and climb those mountains. There is no doubt that salvation is worth all that effort; but we do not obtain it by our works. It is "to him that worketh not, but believeth" (Rom. 5:5). We work because we are saved; we do not work to be saved. We work from the cross; but not towards it. It is written, "Work out your own salvation with fear and trembling" (Phil. 2:12). Why, you must have your salvation before you can work it out. Suppose I say to my little boy, "I want you to spend that hundred dollars carefully." "Well," he says, "let me have the hundred dollars; and I will be careful how I spend it." I remember when I first left home and went to Boston; I had spent all my money, and I went to the post-office three times a day. I knew there was only one mail a day from home; but I thought by some possibility there might be a letter for me. At last I received a leter from my little sister; and oh, how glad I was to get it. She had heard that there were a great many pickpockets in Boston, and a large part of that letter was to urge me to be very careful not to let anybody pick my pocket. Now I required to have something in my pocket before I could have it picked. So you must have salvation before you can work it out.

When Christ cried out on Calvary, "It is finished!" He meant what He said. All that men have to do now is just to accept of the work of Jesus Christ. There is no hope for man or woman so long as they are trying to work out salvation for themselves. I can imagine there are some people who will say, as Nicodemus possibly did, "This is a very mysterious thing." I see the scowl on that Pharisee's brow as he says, "How can these things be?" It sounds very strange to his ear. "Born again; born of the Spirit! How can these things be?" A great many people say, "You must reason it out; but if you do not reason it out, do not ask us to believe it." I can imagine a great many people saying that. When you ask me to reason it out, I tell you frankly I cannot do it. "The wind bloweth where it listeth, and thou hearest the sound thereof, but canst not tell whence it cometh and whither it goeth: so is every one that is born of the Spirit" (John 3:8). I do not understand everything about the wind. You ask me to reason it out. I cannot. It may blow due north here, and a hundred miles away due south. I may go up a few hundred feet, and find it blowing in an entirely opposite direction from what it is down here. You ask me to explain these currents of wind; but suppose that, because I cannot explain them, and do not understand them, I were to take my stand and assert, "Oh, there is no such thing as wind." I can imagine some little girl saying, "I know more about it than that man does; often have I heard the wind, and felt it blowing against my face"; and she might say, "Did not the wind blow my umbrella out of my hands the other day? and did I not see it blow a man's hat off in the street? Have I not seen it blow the trees in the forest, and the growing corn in the country?"

You might just as well tell me that there is no such thing as wind, as tell me there is no such thing as a man being born of the Spirit. I have felt the spirit of God working in my heart, just as really and as truly as I have felt the wind blowing in my face. I cannot reason it out. There are a great many things I cannot reason out, but which I believe. I never could reason out the creation. I can see the world, but I cannot tell how God made it out of nothing. But almost every man will admit there was a creative power.

There are a great many thing that I cannot explain and cannot reason out, and yet that I believe. I heard a commercial traveler say that he had heard that the ministry and religion of Jesus Christ were matters of revelation and not of investigation. "When it pleased God to reveal His Son in Me," says Paul (Gal. 1:15, 16). There was a party of young men together, going up the country; and on their journey they made up their minds not to believe anything they could not reason out. An old man heard them; and presently he said, "I heard you say you would not believe anything you could not reason out." "Yes," they said, "that is so." "Well," he said, "coming down on the train to-day, I noticed some geese, some sheep, some swine, and some cattle all eating grass. Can you tell me by what process that same grass was turned into hair, feathers, bristles and wool? Do you believe it is a fact?" "Oh yes," they said, "we cannot help believing that, though we fail to understand it." "Well," said the old man, "I cannot help believing in Jesus Christ." And I cannot help believing in the regeneration of man, when I see men who have been reclaimed, when I see men who have been reformed. Have not some of the very worst men been regenerated — been picked up out of the pit, and had their feet set upon the Rock, and a new song put in their mouths? Their tongues were cursing and blaspheming; and now are occupied in praising God. Old things have passed away, and all things have become new. They are not reformed only, but REGENERATED — new men in Christ Jesus.

Down there in the dark alleys of one of our great cities is a poor drunkard. I think if you want to get near hell, you should go to a poor drunkard's home. Go to the house of that poor miserable drunkard. Is there anything more like hell on earth? See the want and distress that reign there. But hark! A footstep is heard at the door, and the children run and hide themselves. The patient wife waits to meet the man. He has been her torment. Many a time she has borne about the marks of his blows for weeks. Many a time that strong right hand has been brought down on her defenseless head. And now she waits expecting to hear his oaths and suffer his brutal treatment. He comes in and says to her: "I have been to the meeting; and I heard there that if I will I can be converted. I believe that God is able to save me." Go down to that house again in a few weeks: and what a change! As you approach you hear some one singing. It is not the song of a reveller, but the strains of that good old hymn, "Rock of Ages." The children are no longer afraid of the man, but cluster around his knee. His wife is near him, her face lit up with a happy glow. Is not that a picture of Regeneration? I can take you to many such homes, made happy by the regenerating power of the religion of Christ. What men want is the power to overcome temptation, the power to lead a right life.

The only way to get into the kingdom of God is to be "born" into it. The law of this country requires that the President should be born in the country. When foreigners come to our shores they have no right to complain against such a law, which forbids them from ever becoming Presidents. Now, has not God a right to make a law that all those who become heirs of eternal life must be "born" into His kingdom?

An unregenerated man would rather be in hell than in heaven. Take a man whose heart is full of corruption and wickedness, and place him in heaven among the pure, the holy and the redeemed; and he would not want to stay there. Certainly, if we are to be happy in heaven we must begin to make a heaven here on earth. Heaven is a prepared place for a prepared people. If a gambler or a blasphemer were taken out of the streets of New York and placed on the crystal pavement of heaven and under the shadow of the tree of life, he would say, "I do not want to stay here." If men were taken to heaven just as they are by nature, without having their hearts regenerated, there would be another rebellion in heaven. Heaven is filled with a company of those who have been TWICE BORN.

In the 14th and 15th verses of this chapter we read "As Moses lifted up the serpent in the wilderness, even so must the Son of Man be lifted up; that *whosoever* believeth in Him should not perish, but have eternal life." "*Whosoever*." Mark that! Let me tell you who are unsaved what God has done for you. He has done everything that He could do toward your salvation. You need not wait for God to do anything more. In one place he asks the question, what more could he have done (Isa. 5:4). He sent His prophets, and they killed them; then He sent His beloved Son, and they murdered Him. Now He has sent the Holy Spirit to convince us of sin, and to show how we are to be saved.

In this chapter we are told how men are to be saved, namely, by Him who was lifted up on the cross. Just as Moses lifted up the brazen serpent in the wilderness, so must the Son of Man be lifted up, "that whosoever believeth in Him should not perish, but have eternal life." Some men complain and say that it is very unreasonable that they should be held responsible for the sin of a man six thousand years ago. It was not long ago that a man was talking to me about this injustice, as he called it. If a man thinks he is going to answer God in that way, I tell you it will not do him any good. If you are lost, it will not be on account of Adam's sin.

Let me illustrate this; and perhaps you will be better able to understand it. Suppose I am dying of consumption, which I inherited from my father or mother. I did not get the disease by any fault of my own, by any neglect of my health; I inherited it, let us suppose. A friend happens to come along: he looks at me, and says: "Moody, you are in a consumption." I reply, "I know it very well; I do not want any one to tell me that." "But," he says, "there is a remedy." "But, sir, I do not believe it. I have tried the leading physicians in this country and in Europe; and they tell me there is no hope." "But you know me, Moody; you have known me for years." "Yes, sir." "Do you think, then, I would tell you a falsehood?" "No." "Well, ten years ago I was as far gone. I was given up by the physicians to die, but I took this medicine and it cured me. I am perfectly well: look at me." I say that it is "a very strange case." "Yes, it may be strange; but it is a fact. This medicine cured me: take this medicine, and it will cure you. Athough it has cost me a great deal, it shall not cost you anything. Do not make light of it, I beg of you." "Well," I say, "I should like to believe you; but this is contrary to my reason."

Hearing this, my friend goes away and returns with another friend, and that one testifies to the same thing. I am still disbelieving; so he goes away, and brings in another friend, and another, and another; and they all testify to the same thing. They say they were as bad as myself; that they took the same medicine that has been offered to me; and that it has cured them. My friend then hands me the medicine. I dash it to the ground; I do not believe in its saving power; I die. The reason is then that I spurned the remedy. So, if you perish, it will not be because Adam fell; but because you spurned the remedy offered to save you. You will choose darkness rather than light. "How then shall ye escape, if ye neglect so great salvation?" There is no hope for you if you neglect the remedy. It does no good to look at the wound. If we had been in the Israelitish camp and had been bitten by one of the fiery serpents, it would have done us no good to look at the wound. Looking at the wound will never save any one. What you must do is to look at the Remedy—look away to Him who hath power to save you from your sin.

Behold the camp of the Israelites; look at the scene that is pictured to your eyes! Many are dying because they neglect the remedy that is offered. In that arid desert is many a short and tiny grave; many a child has been bitten by the fiery serpents. Fathers and mothers are bearing away their children. Over yonder they are just burying a mother; a loved mother is about to be laid in the earth. All the family, weeping, gather around the beloved form. You hear the mournful cries; you see the bitter tears. The father is being borne away to his last resting place. There is wailing going up all over the camp. Tears are pouring down for thousands who have passed away; thousands more are dying; and the plague is raging from one end of the camp to the other.

I see in one tent an Israelitish mother bending over the form of a beloved boy just coming into the bloom of life, just budding into manhood. She is wiping away the sweat of death that is gathering upon his brow. Yet a little while, and his eyes are fixed and glassy, for life is ebbing fast away. The mother's heart-strings are torn and bleeding. All at once she hears a noise in the camp. A great shout goes up. What does it mean? She goes to the door of the tent. "What is the noise in the camp?" she asks those passing by. And some one says: "Why, my good woman, have you not heard the good news that has come to the camp?" "No," says the woman, "Good news! What is it?" "Why, have you not heard about it? God has provided a remedy." "What! for the bitten Israelites? Oh, tell me what the remedy is!" "Why, God has instructed Moses to make a brazen serpent, and to put it on a pole in the middle of the camp; and He has declared that whosoever looks upon it shall live. The shout that you hear is the shout of the people when they see the serpent lifted up." The mother goes back into the tent, and she says: "My boy, I have good news to tell you. You need not die! My boy, my boy, I have come with good tidings; you can live!" He is already getting stupefied; he is so weak he cannot walk to the door of the tent. She puts her strong arms under him and lifts him up. "Look yonder; look right there under the hill!" But the boy does not see anything; he says—"I do not see anything; what is it, mother?" And she says: "Keep looking, and you will see it." At last he catches a glimpse of the glistening serpent; and lo, he is well! And thus it is with many a young convert. Some men say, "Oh, we do not believe in sudden conversions." How long did it take to cure that boy? How long did it take to cure those serpent-bitten Israelites? It was just a look; and they were well.

That Hebrew boy is a young convert. I can fancy that I see him now calling on all those who were with him to praise God. He sees another young man bitten as he was; and he runs up to him and tells him, "You need not die." "Oh," the young man replies, "I cannot live; it is not possible. There is not a physician in Israel who can cure me." He does not know that he need not die. "Why, have you not heard the news? God has provided a remedy." "What remedy?" "Why, God has told Moses to lift up a brazen serpent, and has said that none of those who look upon that serpent shall die." I can just imagine that young man. He may be what you call an intellectual young man. He says to the young convert: "You do not think I am going to believe anything like that? If the physicians in Israel cannot cure me, how do you think that an old brass serpent on a pole is going to cure me?" "Why, sir, I was as bad as yourself!" "You do not say so!" "Yes, I do." "That is the most astonishing thing I ever heard," says the young man: "I wish you would explain the philosophy of it." "I cannot. I only know that I looked at that serpent, and I was cured: that did it. I just looked; that is all. My mother told me the reports that were being heard through the camp; and I just believed what my mother said, and I am perfectly well." "Well, I do not believe you were bitten as badly as I have been." The young man pulls up his sleeve. "Look there! That mark shows where I was bitten; and I tell you I was worse than you are." "Well, if I understand the philosophy of it I would look and get well." "Let your philosophy go: *look and live.*" "But, sir, you ask me to do an unreasonable thing. If God had said, Take the brass and rub it into the wound, there might be something in the brass that would cure the bite. Young man, explain the philosophy of it." I have often seen people before me who have talked in that way. But the young man calls in another, and takes him into the tent, and says: "Just tell him how the Lord saved you;" and he tells just the same story; and he calls in others, and they all say the same thing.

The young man says it is a very strange thing. "If the Lord had told Moses to go and get some herbs, or roots, and stew them, and take the decoction as a medicine, there would be something in that. But it is so contrary to nature to do such a thing as look at the serpent, that I cannot do it." At length his mother, who has been out in the camp, comes in, and she says, "My boy, I have just the best news in the world for you. I was in the camp, and I saw hundreds who were very far gone, and they are all perfectly well now." The young man says: "I should like to get well; it is a very painful thought to die; I want to go into the promised land, and it is terrible to die here in this wilderness; but the fact is—I do not understand the remedy. It does not appeal to my reason. I cannot believe that I can get well in a moment." And the young man dies in consequence of his own unbelief.

God provided a remedy for this bitten Israelite—"Look and live!" And there is eternal life for every poor sinner. Look, and you can be saved, my reader, this very hour. God has provided a remedy; and it is offered to all. The trouble is, a great many people are looking at the pole. Do not look at the pole; that is the church. You need not look at the church; the church is all right, but the church cannot save you. Look beyond the pole. Look at the Crucified One. Look to Calvary. Bear in mind, sinner, that Jesus died for all. You need not look at ministers; they are just God's chosen instruments to hold up the Remedy, to hold up Christ. And so, my friends, take your eyes off from men; take your eyes off from the church. Lift them up to Jesus; who took away the sin of the world, and there will be life for you from this hour.

Thank God, we do not require an education to teach us how to look. That little girl, that little boy, only four years old, who cannot read, can look. When the father is coming home, the mother says to her little boy, "Look! look! look!" and the little child learns to look long before he is a year old. And that is the way to be saved. It is to look at the Lamb of God "who taketh away the sin of the world;" and there is life this moment for every one who is willing to look.

Some men say, "I wish I knew how to be saved." Just take God at His word and trust His Son this very day—this very hour—this very moment. He will save you, if you will trust Him. I imagine I hear some one saying, "I do not feel the bite as much as I wish I did. I know I am a sinner, and all that; but I do not feel the bite enough." How much does God want you to feel it?

When I was in Belfast I knew a doctor who had a friend, a leading surgeon there; and he told me that the surgeon's custom was, before performing any operation, to say to the patient, "Take a good look at the wound, and then fix your eyes on me; and do not take them off till I get through." I thought at the time that was a good illustration. Sinner, take a good look at your wound; and then fix your eyes on Christ, and do not take them off. It is better to look at the Remedy than at the wound. See what a poor wretched sinner you are; and then look at the Lamb of God who "taketh away the sin of the world." He died for the ungodly and the sinner. Say "I will take Him!" And may God help you to lift your eye to the Man on Calvary. And as the Israelites looked upon the serpent and were healed, so may you look and live.

After the battle of Pittsburgh Landing I was in a hospital at Murfreesbro.' In the middle of the night I was aroused and told that a man in one of the wards wanted to see me. I went to him and he called me "chaplain"—I was not the chaplain—and said he wanted me to help him die. And I said, "I would take you right up in my arms and carry you into the kingdom of God if I could; but I cannot do it: I cannot help you die!" And he said, "Who can?" I said, "The Lord Jesus Christ can— He came for that purpose." He shook his head, and said, "He cannot save me; I have sinned all my life." And I said, "But He came to save sinners." I thought of his mother in the north, and I was sure that she was anxious that he should die in peace; so I resolved I would stay with him. I prayed two or three times, and repeated all the promises I could; for it was evident that in a few hours he would be gone. I said I wanted to read him a conversation that Christ had with a man who was anxious about his soul. I turned to the third chapter of John. His eyes were riveted on me; and when I came to the 14th and 15th verses—the passage before us—he caught up the words, "As Moses lifted up the serpent in the wilderness, even so must the Son of Man be lifted up; that whosoever believeth in Him should not perish, but have eternal life." He stopped me and said, "Is that there?" I said "Yes." He asked me to read it again; and I did so. He leant his elbows on the cot and clasping his hands together, said, "That's good; won't you read it again?" I read it the third time; and then went on with the rest of the chapter. When I had finished, his eyes were closed, his hands were folded, and there was a smile on his face. Oh, how it was lit up! What a change had come over it! I saw his lips quivering, and leaning over him I heard in a faint whisper, "As Moses lifted up the serpent in the wilderness, even so must the Son of Man be lifted up; that whosoever believeth in Him should not perish, but have eternal life." He opened his eyes and said, "That's enough; don't read any more." He lingered a few hours, pillowing his head on those two verses; and then went up in one of Christ's chariots, to take his seat in the kingdom of God.

Christ said to Nicodemus: "Except a man be born again, he cannot see the kingdom of God." You may see many countries;

but there is one country—the land of Beulah, which John Bunyan saw in vision—you shall never behold, unless you are born again—regenerated by Christ. You can look abroad and see many beautiful trees; but the tree of life, you shall never behold, unless your eyes are made clear by faith in the Saviour. You may see the beautiful rivers of the earth—you may ride upon their bosoms; but bear in mind that your eye will never rest upon the river which bursts out from the Throne of God and flows through the upper Kingdom, unless you are born again. God has said it, and not man. You will never see the kingdom of God except you are born again. You may see the kings and lords of the earth; but the King of kings and Lord of lords you will never see except you are born again. When you are in London you may go to the Tower and see the crown of England, which is worth thousands of dollars, and is guarded there by soldiers; but bear in mind that your eye will never rest upon the crown of life except you are born again.

You may hear the songs of Zion which are sung here; but one song—that of Moses and the Lamb—the uncircumcised ear shall never hear; its melody will only gladden the ear of those who have been born again. You may look upon the beautiful mansions of earth, but bear in mind the mansions which Christ has gone to prepare you shall never see unless you are born again. It is God who says it. You may see ten thousand beautiful things in this world; but the city that Abraham caught a glimpse of — and from that time became a pilgrim and sojourner — you shall never see unless you are born again (Heb. 11:8, 10-16). You may often be invited to marriage feasts here; but you will never attend the marriage supper of the Lamb except you are born again. It is God who says it, dear friend. You may be looking on the face of your sainted mother to-night; and feel that she is praying for you; but the time will come when you shall never see her more unless you are born again.

The reader may be a young man or a young lady who has

recently stood by the bedside of a dying mother; and she may have said, "Be sure and meet me in heaven," and you made the promise. Ah! you shall never see her more, except you are born again. I believe Jesus of Nazareth, sooner than those infidels who say you do not need to be born again. Parents, if you hope to see your children who have gone before, you must be born of the Spirit. Possibly you are a father or a mother who has recently borne a loved one to the grave; and how dark your home seems! Never more will you see your child, unless you are born again. If you wish to be re-united to your loved one, you must be born again. I may be addressing a father or a mother who has a loved one up yonder. If you could hear that loved one's voice, it would say, "Come this way." Have you a sainted friend up yonder? Young man or young lady, have you not a mother in the world of light? If you could hear her speak, would not she say, "Come this way, my son,"—"Come this way, my daughter?" If you would ever see her more you must be born again.

We all have an Elder Brother there. Nearly nineteen hundred years ago He crossed over, and from the heavenly shores He is calling you to heaven. Let us turn our backs upon the world. Let us give a deaf ear to the world. Let us look to Jesus on the Cross and be saved. Then we shall one day see the King in His beauty, and we shall go no more out.

WHEN A MAN SOWS, HE EXPECTS TO REAP

Notice these four things about sowing and reaping: A man expects to reap when he sows; he expects to reap the same kind of seed that he sows; he expects to reap more; and ignorance of the kind of seed makes no difference.

First: *When a man sows, he expects to reap.*

If a farmer went on sowing, spring after spring, and never reaping in the autumn, you would say he was a fit subject for the lunatic asylum. No; he is always looking forward to the time when he will reap the reward of his toil. He never expects that the seed he has sown will be lost.

A young man serves a long apprenticeship to some trade or profession; but he expects by and by to reap the fruit of all those years of patient industry. Ask an engineer why he works so hard for five, six, or seven years in the endeavor to learn his profession. He replies that he is looking forward to the reaping time, when his fortune and reputation will be made. The lawyer studies long and hard; but he, too, anticipates the time when his clients will be numerous, and he will be repaid for his toil. A great many medical students have a hard time trying to support themselves while they are at college. As soon as they get their diploma and become doctors they expect that the reaping time is coming; that is what they have been working for.

Some harvests ripen almost immediately, but as a rule we find it true in the natural world that *there is delay* before the seed comes to maturity. It is growing all the time, however; first

107

the little green shoot breaking through the soil, then the blade, then the ear, then the full corn in the ear. The farmer is not disappointed because all his crops do not spring up in a night like mushrooms. He looks forward with patience, knowing that the reaping time will come in due season.

So with the harvest of our actions. Few men, if any, would indulge in sin unless they expected pleasure out of it. A drunkard does not drink for the mere sake of drinking, but in the hope of present enjoyment. A thief does not steal for the mere sake of stealing, but for the sake of gain. And similarly with the good man. He does not make sacrifices merely for the sake of sacrifice, but because thereby he hopes and expects to do good, and help others. All these things are means to ends: there is always expectation of a harvest.

THE CERTAINTY OF THE REAPING

The text bids us look forward to the certainty of the reaping: "Whatsoever a man soweth, that *shall* he also reap."

We know what it is to have a failure of the crops, but in the spiritual world no such failure is possible. Wet soil may rot the seed, or frost may nip the early buds, or the weather may prove too wet or too dry to bring the crops to maturity, but none of these things occur to prevent the harvest of one's actions. The Bible tells us that God will render to every man according to his deeds. "To them who by patient continuance in well-doing seek for glory and honor and immortality, eternal life: but unto them that are contentious, and do not obey the truth, but obey unrighteousness, indignation and wrath, tribulation and anguish upon every soul of man that doeth evil." How careful we should be of our actions in all departments of our being, physical, moral, intellectual! The deeds we do, the words we speak, the thoughts we harbor, are all recorded, and shall meet their just reward, for God is no respecter of persons.

And it must not be overlooked that *the harvest comes as a*

necessary consequence of the sowing. It has been said that God is not a sort of a moral despot, as He is so frequently regarded. He does not sit on a throne, attaching penalties to particular actions as they come up for judgment. He has laid down certain laws, of which the law of sowing and reaping is one, and punishment is the natural outcome of sin. There is no escape. It must be borne; and though others may have to reap *with* you, no one can reap *for* you.

The text teaches, further, that *the harvest is one or other of two kinds.* There are two, and only two, directions in which the law leads. Sowing to the flesh, and a harvest of corruption —sowing to the Spirit, and a harvest of everlasting life.

SOWING TO THE FLESH

"Sowing to the flesh" does not mean simply taking due care of the body. The body was made in the image of God, and the body of a believer is a temple of the Holy Ghost, and we may be sure that due care for the image is well-pleasing to God. The expression refers rather to pandering to the lusts of the body, pampering it, providing gratification for its unlawful desires at the expense of the higher part of a man, indulging the animal propensities which in their excess are sinful. "Sowing to the flesh" is scattering the seeds of selfishness, which always must yield a harvest of corruption.

"When we were in the flesh, the motions of sins did work in our members to bring forth fruit unto death." And what does Paul say are the works of the flesh? "Adultery, fornication, uncleanness, lasciviousness, idolatry, witchcraft, hatred, variance, emulations, wrath, strife, seditions, heresies, envyings, murders, drunkenness, revellings, and such like."

I was at the Paris exhibition in 1867, and I noticed there a little oil painting, only about a foot square, and the face was the most hideous I have ever seen. On the paper attached to the painting were the words "Sowing the tares," and the face looked more like a demon's than a man's. As he sowed these tares, up came serpents and reptiles, and they were crawling up on his body, and all around were woods with wolves and animals prowling in them. I have seen that picture many times since. Ah! the reaping time is coming. If you sow to the flesh you must reap the flesh. If you sow to the wind you must reap the whirlwind.

And yet it must not be thought that indulgence in the grosser vices is the only way of sowing to the flesh. Every desire, every action that has not God for its end and object is seed sown to the flesh. If a man is sowing for a harvest of money or ambition, he is sowing to the flesh, and will reap corruption, just as surely as the liar and adulterer. No matter how "polite" and "refined" and "respectable" the seed may be, no matter how closely it resembles the good seed, its true nature will out, the blight of corruption will be upon it.

How foolish are the strivings of men in view of this judgment! Many a man will sacrifice time, health—even his character—for money. What does he gain? *Corruption;* something that is not eternal, that has not the qualities of "everlasting life." John said, "The world passeth away, and the lust thereof." Peter said, "All flesh is as grass, and all the glory of man as the flower of grass. The grass withereth, and the flower thereof falleth away." None of these fleshly things have their roots in the eternal. You may even outlive them in your own short life.

NO BRIDGE BETWEEN

Now, men make this mistake—they sow to the flesh, and they think they will reap the harvest of the spirit; and on the other hand, they sow to the spirit and are disappointed when they do not reap a temporal harvest.

A teacher had been relating to his class the parable of the rich man and Lazarus, and he asked:

"Now, which would you rather be, boys, the rich man or Lazarus?"

One boy answered, "I would rather be the rich man while I live, and Lazarus when I die."

That cannot be; it is flesh and corruption, or, Spirit and everlasting life. There is no bridge from one to the other.

"Seed which is sown for a spiritual harvest has no tendency whatever to procure temporal well-being. Christ declared, 'Blessed are the pure in heart; for they shall see God; blessed are they that hunger and thirst after righteousness, for they shall be filled' (with righteousness); 'blessed are they that mourn, for they shall be comforted.' You observe the beatific vision of the Almighty—fulness of righteousness—divine comfort. There is nothing earthly here, it is spiritual results for spiritual labor. It is not said that the pure in heart shall be made rich; or that they who hunger and thirst after righteousness shall be filled with bread, or that they who mourn shall rise in life, and obtain distinction. Each department has its own appropriate harvest, reserved exclusively to its own method of sowing.

"Everything reaps its own harvest, every act has its own reward. And before you covet the enjoyment which another possesses, you must first calculate the cost at which it was procured.

"For instance, the religious tradesman complains that his honesty is a hindrance to his success; that the tide of custom pours into the doors of his less scrupulous neighbor in the same street, while he himself waits for hours idle. My brother, do you think that God is going to reward honor, integrity, high-mindedness, with this world's coin? Do you fancy that He will pay spiritual excellence with plenty of custom? Now consider the price that man has paid for his success. Perhaps mental degradation and inward dishonor. His advertisements are all deceptive, his treatment of his workmen tyrannical, his cheap prices made possible by inferior articles. Sow that man's seed, and you will reap that man's harvest. Cheat, lie, be unscrupulous in your assertions, and custom will come to you. But if the price be too high, let him have his harvest, and you take yours—a clear conscience, a pure mind, rectitude within and without. Will you part with that for his harvest?"

SOWING TO THE SPIRIT

"Sowing to the Spirit" implies self-denial, resistance of evil, obedience to the Spirit, walking in the Spirit, living in the Spirit, guidance by the Spirit. We sow to the Spirit when we use our abilities and means to advance Spiritual things; when we support and encourage those who are extending the influence of the Spirit. We sow to the Spirit when we crucify the flesh and all its lusts, when we yield ourselves to Him as we once yielded ourselves to the flesh. A Jewish rabbi once said: "There are in every man two impulses, good and evil. He who offers God his evil impulses offers the best sacrifice."

The fruit of such sowing is "love, joy, peace, long-suffering, gentleness, goodness, faith, meekness, temperance."

In this world the harvest is growth of character, deeper respect, increasing usefulness to others; in the next world, acceptance with God, everlasting life.

Among the last recorded words of Henry Lloyd Garrison in his public speeches in England were these: "I began my advocacy of the anti-slavery cause in the Northern States of America, in the midst of the brickbats and rotten eggs; and I ended it on the soil of South Carolina almost literally buried beneath the wreaths of flowers which were heaped upon me by her liberated bondmen."

A young man was employed by a large commission firm in New York City during the late civil war, to negotiate with a certain party for a lot of damaged beans. The beans were purchased, delivered, and spread out upon the upper floor of the building occupied by the firm.

Men were employed to turn them over and over, and to

sprinkle them with a solution of soda, so as to improve their appearance and render them more salable. A large lot of the first quality of beans was then purchased; some of the good beans were first put into barrels, then the barrels were nearly filled with the poor ones; after this the good ones were again put on the top and the barrels headed up for sale.

The employer marked the barrels, "Beans—A 1." The clerk seeing this, said: "Do you think, sir, that it is right to mark these beans A 1?"

The employer retorted sharply: "Are you head of the firm?"

The clerk said no more. The barreling and heading went on. When all was ready, the beans (many hundreds of barrels) were put on the market for sale. Specimens of the best quality were shown in the office to buyers.

At length a shrewd purchaser came in (no man is so sharp in business but he will often meet his equal), examined the samples in the office, inquired the price, and then wished to see the stock in bulk. The clerk was ordered to go with the buyer to the upper loft and show him the stock. An open barrel was shown apparently of the same quality of the sample. The buyer then said to the clerk:

"Young man, the samples of beans shown me are of the first quality, and it is impossible to purchase beans anywhere in the market for the price at which you offer them; there is something wrong here. Tell me, are these beans the same quality throughout the entire barrel as they appear on the top?"

The clerk now found himself in a strange position. He thought, "Shall I lie for my employer, as he undoubtedly means I shall; or shall I tell the truth, come what will?" He decided for the truth, and said:

"No, sir, they are not."

"Then," said the customer. "I do not want them"; and he left.

The clerk entered the office. The employer said to him: "Did you sell that man those beans?"

He said, "No, sir."

"Why not?"

"Well, sir, the man asked me if those beans were of the same quality through the entire barrel as they appeared on the top. I told him they were not. He then said: 'I do not want them,' and left."

"Go to the cashier," said the employer, "and get your wages; we want you no longer."

He received his pay and left the office, rejoicing that he had not lied for the purposes of abetting a sordid avariciousness, and benefiting an unprincipled employer.

Three weeks after this the firm sent after the young clerk, entreated him to come back again into their employ, and offered him three hundred dollars salary more per year than they had ever before given him.

And thus was his honesty and truthfulness rewarded. The firm knew and felt that the man was right, although apparently they had lost largely by his honesty. They wished to have him again in their employ, because they knew that they could trust him, and never suffer through fraud and deception. They knew that their financial interests would be safe in his custody. They respected and honored that young man.

THE LESSON OF PATIENCE

Let us learn the lesson of patience. "Behold the husbandman waiteth for the precious fruit of the earth, and hath long patience for it, until he received the early and latter rain." Delay does not mean denial. Too often one generation sows and another has to reap. God is a jealous God, "visiting the iniquity of the fathers upon the children unto the third and fourth generation of them that hate" Him.

In the early years of Israel's existence as a separate people, God commanded them to give the land of Canaan rest every seventh year.

"Six years thou shalt sow thy land, and shalt gather in the fruits thereof: but the seventh year thou shalt let it rest and lie still; that the poor of thy people may eat, and what they leave the beasts of the field shall eat. In like manner thou shalt deal with thy vineyard, and with thy olive yard." From the anointing of Saul to be king this law was not observed. After four hundred and ninety years God gave the nation into captivity for seventy years. During this period the land had rest; seventy sabbath years to compensate for the sabbath years of which it had been deprived. Those Israelites sowed the bitter seed of disobedience, and their descendants had to reap the harvest in exile and captivity.

A leading surgeon performed a critical operation before his class one day. The operation was successful, as far as his part was concerned. But he turned to the class and said: "Six years ago a wise way of living might have prevented this disease. Two years ago a safe and simple operation might have cured it. We have done our best to-day as the case now stands, but Nature will have her word to say. She does not always repeal her capital sentences." Next day the patient died, reaping the fruit of his excesses.

Paul says: "Let us not be weary in well-doing; in due season we shall reap if we faint not."

In a recent chat with an interviewer, Mr. Edison quite unconsciously preached a most powerful sermon on perseverance and patience.

He described his repeated efforts to make the phonograph reproduce the aspirated sound, and added: "For eighteen to twenty hours a day for the last seven months I have worked on this single word 'specia.' I said into the phonograph, 'specia, specia, specia,' but the instrument responded, 'pecia, pecia, pecia.' It was enough to drive one mad! But I held firm, and I have succeeded."

An insurance case was brought to Daniel Webster when he

was a young lawyer in Portsmouth. Only a small amount was involved, and a twenty-dollar fee was all that was promised. He saw that to do his client full justice, a journey to Boston would be desirable, in order to consult the law library. He would be out of pocket by the expedition, and for the time he would receive no adequate compensation. But he determined to do his best, cost what it might. He accordingly went to Boston and looked up the authorities, and gained the case.

Years after, Webster, who had meanwhile become famous, was passing through New York. An important insurance case was to be tried that day, and one of the counsel had suddenly been taken ill. Money was no object, and Webster was begged to name his terms and conduct the case.

"I told them," said Mr. Webster, "that it was preposterous to expect me to prepare a legal argument at a few hours' notice. They insisted, however, that I should look at the papers; and this I finally consented to do. It was my old twenty-dollar case over again; and as I never forget anything, I had all the authorities at my fingers' ends. The court knew that I had no time to prepare, and were astonished at the range of my acquirements. So you see, I was handsomely repaid both in fame and money for that journey to Boston; and the moral is that good work is rewarded in the end."

Two men were digging in California for gold. They worked a good deal and got nothing. At last one of them threw down his tools and said:

"I will leave here before we starve"; and he left.

The next day his comrade's patience was rewarded by finding a nugget that supported him until he made a fortune.

"Because sentence against an evil work is not executed speedily, therefore the heart of the sons of men is fully set in them to do evil. Though a sinner do evil an hundred times, and his days be prolonged, yet surely I know that it shall be well with them that fear God, which fear before Him; but it shall not be well with the wicked, neither shall he prolong his days, which are as a shadow; because he feareth not before God."

The idea that because a person does a thing in the dark it will never be brought to light, is fatal—God says it *shall* be brought to light. It is folly for a man who has covered his sins to think there shall be no resurrection of them and no final adjudication. Look at the sons of Jacob. They sold Joseph and deceived their father. Twenty long years rolled away, and away down to Egypt their sin followed them; for they said: "We are guilty of the blood of our brother." The reaping time had come at last, for those ten boys who sold their brother.

I was once preaching in Chicago, and a woman who was nearly out of her mind came to me. You know there are some people who mock at religious meetings, and say that religion drives people mad. It is *sin* that drives people mad. It is the want of Christ that sinks people into despair. This was the woman's story: She had a family of children. One of her neighbors had died, and her husband had brought home a little child. She said, "I don't want the child," but her husband said, "You must take it and look after it." She said she had enough to do with her own, and she told her husband to take that child away. But he would not. She confessed that she tried to starve the child; but it lingered on. One night it cried all night; I suppose it wanted food. At last she took the clothes and threw them over the child, and smothered it. No one saw her; no one knew anything about it. The child was buried. Years had passed away; and she said, "I hear the voice of that child day and night. It has driven me nearly mad." No one saw the act; but God had seen it, and this retribution followed it. History is full of these things. You need not go to the Bible to find out.

THE FIRST COMMANDMENT

Thou shalt have no other gods before me.

MY FRIEND, are you ready to be weighed against the commandment? Have you fulfilled, or are you willing to fulfil, all the requirements of this law? Put it into one of the scales, and step into the other. Is your heart set upon God alone? Have you no other God? Do you love Him above father or mother, the wife of your bosom, your children, home or land, wealth or pleasure?

If men were true to this commandment, obedience to the remaining nine would follow naturally. It is because they are unsound in this that they break the others.

FEELING AFTER GOD

Philosophers are agreed that even the most primitive races of mankind reach out beyond the world of matter to a superior Being. It is as natural for man to feel after God as it is for the ivy to feel after a support. Hunger and thirst drive him to seek for food, and there is a hunger of the soul that needs satisfying, too. Man does not need to be commanded to worship, as there is not a race so high or so low in the scale of civilization but has some kind of a god. What he needs is to be directed aright.

This is what the first commandment is for. Before we can worship intelligently, we must know what or whom to worship. God does not leave us in ignorance. When Paul went to Athens, he found an altar dedicated to "An Unknown God," and he proceeded to tell of Him whom we worship. When God gave the commandments to Moses, He commenced with a declaraation of His own character, and demanded exclusive recognition. "I am the Lord thy God, which have brought thee out of the land of Egypt, out of the house of bondage. Thou shalt have no other gods before me."

The Rev. Dr. Dale says these words have great significance. "The Jews knew Jehovah as the God who had held back the waves like a wall while they fled across the sea to escape the vengeance of their enemies; they knew Him as the God who had sent thunder, and lightning, and hail, plagues on cattle, and plagues on men, to punish the Egyptians and to compel them to let the children of Israel go; they knew Him as the God whose angel had slain the firstborn of their oppressors, and filled the land from end to end with death, and agony, and terror. He was the same God, so Moses and Aaron told them, who by visions and voices, in promises and precepts, had revealed Himself long before to Abraham, Isaac, and Jacob. We learn what men are from what they say and from what they do. A biography of Luther gives a more vivid and trustworthy knowledge of the man than the most philosophical essay on his character and creed. The story of his imprisonment and of his journey to Worms, his Letters, his Sermons, and his Table-Talk, are worth more than the most elaborate speculations about him. The Jews learned what God is, not from theological dissertations on the Divine attributes, but from the facts of a Divine history. They knew Him for themselves in His own acts and His own words."

Some one asked an Arab: "How do you know that there is a God?" "How do I know whether a man or a camel passed my tent last night?" he replied. God's footprints in nature and in our own experience are the best evidence of His existence and character.

THE ISRAELITES WERE EXPOSED TO DANGER

Remember to whom this commandment was given, and we shall see further how necessary it was. The forefathers of the Israelites had worshipped idols, not many generations back. They had recently been delivered out of Egypt, a land of many gods. The Egyptians worshipped the sun, the moon, insects, animals, etc. The ten plagues were undoubtedly meant by God to bring confusion upon many of their sacred objects. The children of Israel were going up to take possession of a land that was inhabited by heathen, who also worshipped idols. There was therefore great need of such a commandment as this. There could be no right relationship between God and man in those days any more than to-day, until man understood that he must recognize God alone, and not offer Him a divided heart.

If He created us, He certainly ought to have our homage. Is it not right that He should have the first and only place in our affections?

NO COMPROMISE

This is one matter in which no toleration can be shown. Religious liberty is a good thing, within certain limits. But it is one thing to show toleration to those who agree on essentials, and another, to those who differ on fundamental beliefs. They were willing to admit any god to the Roman Pantheon. One reason why the early Christians were persecuted was that they would not accept a place for Jesus Christ there. Napoleon is said to have entertained the idea of having separate temples in Paris for every known religion, so that every stranger should have a place of worship when attracted toward that city. Such plans are directly opposed to the Divine one. God sounded no uncertain note in this commandment. It is plain, unmistakable, uncompromising.

We may learn a lesson from the way a farmer deals with the little shoots that spring up around the trunk of an apple tree. They look promising, and one who has not learned better might welcome their growth. But the farmer knows that they will draw the life-sap from the main tree, injuring its prospects so that it will produce inferior fruit. He therefore takes his axe and his hoe, and cuts away these suckers. The tree then gives a more plentiful and a finer crop.

GOD'S PRUNING KNIFE

"Thou shalt not" is the pruning-knife that God uses. From beginning to end, the Bible calls for whole-hearted allegiance to Him. There is to be no compromise with other gods.

It took long years for God to impress this lesson upon the Israelites. He called them to be a chosen nation. He made them a peculiar people. But you will notice in Bible history that they turned away from Him continually, and were punished with plague, pestilence, war and famine. Their sin was not that they renounced God altogether, but that they wanted to worship other gods beside Him. Take the case of Solomon as an example of the whole nation. He married heathen wives who turned away his heart after other gods, and built high places for their idols, and lent countenance to their worship. That was the history of frequent turnings of the whole nation away from God, until finally He sent them into captivity in Babylon and kept them there for seventy years. Since then the Jews have never returned to other gods.

Hasn't the church to contend with the same difficulty to-day? There are very few who in their hearts do not believe in God, but what they will not do is give Him exclusive right of way. Missionaries tell us that they could easily get converts if they did not require them to be baptized, thus publicly renouncing their idols. Many a person in our land would become a Christian if the gate was not so strait. Christianity is too strict for them. They are not ready to promise full allegiance to God alone. Many a professing Christian is a stumbling-block because his worship is divided. On Sunday he worships God; on week days God has little or no place in his thoughts.

FALSE GODS IN AMERICA TODAY

You don't have to go to heathen lands to-day to find false gods. America is full of them. Whatever you make most of is your god. Whatever you love more than God is your idol. Many a man's heart is like some Kaffirs' huts, so full of idols that there is hardly room to turn around. Rich and poor, learned and un-learned, all classes of men and women are guilty of this sin. "The mean man boweth down, and the great man humbleth himself."

A man may make a god of himself, of a child, of a mother, of some precious gift that God has bestowed upon him. He may forget the Giver, and let his heart go out in adoration toward the gift.

Many make a god of pleasure; that is what their hearts are set on. If some old Greek or Roman came to life again and saw men in a drunken debauch, would he believe that the worship of Bacchus had died out? If he saw the streets of our large cities filled with harlots, would be believe that the worship of Venus had ceased?

Others take fashion as their god. They give their time and thought to dress. They fear what others will think of them. Do not let us flatter ourselves that all idolaters are in heathen countries.

With many it is the god of money. We haven't got through worshipping the golden calf yet. If a man will sell his principles for gold, isn't he making it a god? If he trusts in his wealth to keep him from want and to supply his needs, are not riches his god? Many a man says, "Give me money, and I will give you heaven. What care I for all the glories and treasures of heaven? Give me treasures here! I don't care for heaven! I want to be a successful business man." How true are the words of

Job: "If I have made gold my hope, or have said to the fine gold, Thou art my confidence; if I rejoiced because my wealth was great, and because mine hand had begotten much; if I beheld the sun when it shined, or the moon walking in brightness; and my heart hath been secretly enticed, or my mouth hath kissed my hand: this also were an iniquity to be punished by the judge: for I should have denied the God that is above."

But all false gods are not as gross as these. There is *the atheist.* He says that he does not believe in God; he denies His existence, but he can't help setting up some other god in His place. Voltaire said, "If there were no God, it would be necessary to invent one." So the atheist speaks of the Great Unknown, the First Cause, the Infinite Mind, etc. Then there is *the deist.* He is a man who believes in one God who caused all things: but he doesn't believe in revelation. He only accepts such truths as can be discovered by reason. He doesn't believe in Jesus Christ, or in the inspiration of the Bible. Then there is *the pantheist,* who says: "I believe that the whole universe is God. He is in the air, the water, the sun, the stars"; the liar and the thief included.

MOSES' FAREWELL MESSAGE

Let me call your attention to a verse in the thirty-second chapter of Deuteronomy, thirty-first verse: "For their rock is not as our Rock, even our enemies themselves being judges."

These words were uttered by Moses, in his farewell address to Israel. He had been with them forty years. He was their leader and instructor. All the blessings of heaven came to them through him. And now the old man is about to leave them. If you have never read his speech, do so. It is one of the best sermons in print. I know few sermons in the Old or New Testament that compare with it.

I can see Moses as he delivers this address. His natural activity has not abated. He still has the vigor of youth. His long white hair flows over his shoulders, and his venerable beard covers his breast. He throws down the challenge: "Their rock is not as our Rock, even our enemies themselves being judges."

Has the human heart ever been satisfied with these false gods? Can pleasure or riches fill the soul that is empty of God? How about the atheist, the deist, the pantheist? What do they look forward to? Nothing! Man's life is full of trouble; but when the billows of affliction and disappointment are rising and rolling over them, they have no God to call upon. "They shall cry unto the gods unto whom they offer incense; but they shall not save them at all in the time of their trouble." Therefore I contend "their rock is not as our Rock."

My friends, when the hour of affliction comes, they call in a minister to give consolation. When I was settled in Chicago, I used to be called out to attend many funerals. I would inquire what the man was in his belief. If I found out he was an atheist, or a deist, or a pantheist, when I went to the funeral and in the presence of his friends said one word about that man's doctrine, they would feel insulted. Why is it that in a trying hour, when they have been talking all the time against God — why is it that in the darkness of affliction they call in believers in that God to administer consolation? Why doesn't the atheist preach no hereafter, no heaven, no God, in the hour of affliction? This very fact is an admission that "their rock is not as our Rock, even our enemies themselves being judges."

The deist says there is no use in praying, because nothing can change the decrees of deity; God never answers prayer. Is his rock as our Rock?

The Bible is true. There is only one God. How many men have said to me: "Mr. Moody, I would give the world if I had your faith, your consolation, the hope you have with your religion."

Isn't that a proof that their rock is not as our Rock?

Some years ago I went into a man's house, and when I commenced to talk about religion he turned to his daughter and said: "You had better leave the room. I want to say a few words to Mr. Moody." When she had gone, he opened a perfect torrent of infidelity upon me. "Why did you send your daughter out of the room before you said this?" I asked. "Well," he replied, "I did not think it would do here any good to hear what I said."

Is this rock as our Rock? Would he have sent his daughter out if he really believed what he said?

NO CONSOLATION EXCEPT IN GOD

No. There is no satisfaction for the soul except in the God of the Bible. We come back to Paul's words, and get consolation for time and eternity: — "We know that an idol is nothing in the world, and that there is none other God but one. For though there be that are called gods, whether in heaven or in earth, (as there be gods many, and lords many,) yet to us there is but one God, the Father, of whom are all things, and we in Him; and one Lord Jesus Christ, by whom are all things, and we by Him."

My friend, can you say that sincerely? Is all your hope centered on God in Christ? Are you trusting Him alone? Are you ready to step into the scales and be weighted against this first commandment?

WHOLE-HEARTED ALLEGIANCE

God will not accept a divided heart. He must be absolute monarch. There is not room in your heart for two thrones. Christ said: "No man can serve two masters; for either he will hate the one and love the other, or else he will hold to the one and despise the other. Ye cannot serve God and Mammon." Mark you, He did not say — "No man *shall* serve.... Ye *shall* not serve ...", but "No man *can* serve.... Ye *can* not serve...." That means more than a command; it means that you cannot mix the worship of the true God with the worship of another god any more than you can mix oil and water. It cannot be done.

There is not room for any other throne in the heart if Christ is there. If worldliness should come in, godliness would go out.

The road to heaven and the road to hell lead in different directions. Which master will you choose to follow? Be an out-and-out Christian. "Him only shalt thou serve." Only thus can you be well pleasing to God. The Jews were punished with seventy years of captivity because they worshipped false gods. They have suffered nearly nineteen hundred years because they rejected the Messiah. Will you incur God's displeasure by rejecting Christ too? He died to save you. Trust Him with your whole heart, for with the heart man believeth unto righteousness.

I believe that when Christ has the first place in our hearts — when the kingdom of God is first in everything — we shall have power, and we shall not have power until we give Him His rightful place. If we let some false god come in and steal our love away from the God of heaven, we shall have no peace or power.

CHRIST SEEKING SINNERS

The Son of man came to seek and to save that which was lost.
— Luke 19:10

To me this is one of the sweetest verses in the whole Bible. In this one little short sentence we are told what Christ came into this world for. He came for a purpose, He came to do a work; and in this little verse the whole story is told. He came not to condemn the world, but that the world through Him might be saved.

A few years ago the Prince of Wales came to America, and there was great excitement. The papers took it up, and began to discuss it, and a great many were wondering what he came for. Was it to look into the republican form of government? Was it for his health? Was it to see our institutions? or for this, or for that? He came and went, but he never told us what he came for. But when the Prince of heaven came down into this world, He told us what He came for. God sent Him, and He came to do the will of His Father. What was that? "To seek and to save that which was lost."

You cannot find any place in Scripture where a man was sent by God to do a work in which he failed. God sent Moses to Egypt to bring three millions of bondmen out of the house of bondage into the Promised Land. Did he fail? It looked, at first, as if he were going to. If we had been in the Court when Pharaoh said to Moses, "Who is God, that I should obey Him?" and ordered him out of his presence, we might have thought it meant failure. But did it? God sent Elijah to stand before Ahab, and it was a bold thing when he told him there should be neither dew nor rain; but didn't he lock up the heavens for three years and six months? Now here is God sending His own beloved Son from His bosom, from the throne, down into this world. Do you think He is going to fail? Thanks be to God, He can save to the uttermost, and there is not a man in the world who may not find it so, if he is willing to be saved.

I find a great blessing to myself in taking up a passage like this, and looking all round it, to see what brought it out. If you look back to the close of the eighteenth chapter, you will find Christ coming near the city of Jericho. Sitting by the wayside was a poor, blind beggar. Perhaps he had been there for years, led out, it may be, by one of his children, or perhaps, as we sometimes see, he had a dog to lead him out. There he had sat for years, and his cry had been, "Please give a poor blind man some money." One day, as he was sitting there, a man came down from Jerusalem, and seeing him, took his seat by his side, and said, "Bartimeus, I have good news for you." "What is it?" said the blind beggar. "There is a man in Israel who is able to give you sight." "Oh no," said the blind beggar, "there is no chance of my ever receiving sight. I was born blind, and nobody born blind ever got sight. I shall never see in this world. I may in the world to come, but I must go through this world blind." "But," said the man, "let me tell you. I was at Jerusalem the other day, and the great Galilean prophet was there, and I saw a man who was born blind that had received his sight; and I never saw a man with better sight. He does not need to use glasses. He can see quite clearly." Then for the first time, hope rose in the poor man's heart, and he asked, "How was it done?" "Why, Jesus spat on the ground and made some clay, and anointed his eyes," (that is enough to put a man's sight out, even if he can see!) "and sent him to wash in the pool of Siloam; and while he was doing so he got two good eyes. Yes, it is so.

I talked with him, and I didn't see a man in all Jerusalem who had better sight." "What did he charge?" said Bartimeus. "Nothing. There was no fee or doctor's bill. He got his sight for nothing. You just tell Him what you want; you don't need to have an influential committee to call on Him, or any important deputation. The poor have as much influence with Him as the rich; all are alike." "What is His name?" asked Bartimeus. "Jesus of Nazareth; and if He ever comes this way, don't let Him by without getting your case laid before Him." And the blind man said, "That you may be sure of. He shall never pass this way without my seeking Him."

A day or two after, he was led out, and took his seat at the usual place, still crying out for money. All at once, he heard the footsteps of a coming multitude, and asked, "Who is it? Tell me, who is it?" Some one said it was Jesus of Nazareth that was passing by. The moment he heard that, he said to himself, "Why, that is the man who gives sight to the blind," and he lifted up his cry, "Jesus, thou son of David, have mercy upon me!" I don't know who it was — perhaps it was Peter — who said to him, "Hush! keep still." He thought the Lord was going up to Jerusalem to be crowned king, and he would not like to be disturbed by a poor blind beggar.

Oh, they did not know the Son of God when He was here! He would hush every harp in heaven to hear a sinner pray; no music delights Him so much.

But Bartimeus lifted up his voice louder, "Thou Son of David, have mercy on me." His prayer reached the ear of the Son of God, as prayer always will, and His footsteps were arrested. He told them to bring the man. "Bartimeus," they said, "be of good cheer. Arise, He calleth thee"; and He never called anyone, but He had something good in store for him. Oh, sinner! remember that. They led the blind man to Jesus. The Lord said, "What shall I do for you?" "Lord, that I may receive my sight."

"You shall have it," the Lord said; and straightway his eyes were opened.

I should have liked to have been there, to see that wonderful scene. The first object that met his gaze was the Son of God Himself, and now among the shouting multitude, no one shouts louder than the poor blind man that has got his sight. He glorifies God, and I fancy I can hear him shouting, "Hosanna to the Son of David."

Pardon me, if I now draw a little on my imagination. Bartimeus gets into Jericho, and he says, "I will go and see my wife, and tell her about it." A young convert always wants to talk to his friends about salvation. Away he goes down the street, and he meets a man who passes him, goes on a few yards, and then turns round and says, "Bartimeus, is that you?" "Yes." "Well, I thought it was, but I could not believe my eyes. How have you got your sight?" "Oh, I just met Jesus of Nazareth outside the city, and asked Him to have mercy on me." "Jesus of Nazareth! What, is He in this part of the country?" "Yes. He is right here in Jericho. He is now going down to the western gate." "I should like to see Him," says the man, and away he runs down the street; but he cannot catch a glimpse of Him, even though he stands on tip-toe, being little of stature, and on account of the great throng around Him. "Well," he says, "I am not going to be disappointed"; so he runs on, and climbs up into a sycamore tree. "If I can get on to that branch, hanging right over the highway, He cannot pass without my getting a good look at Him."

That must have been a very strange sight to see the rich man climbing up a tree like a boy, and hiding among the leaves, where he thought nobody would see him, to get a glimpse of the passing stranger!

There comes the crowd bursting out, and he looks for Jesus. He looks at Peter; "That's not He." He looks at John; "That's not He." At last his eye rests on One fairer than the sons of men; "That's He!" and Zaccheus, just peeping out from among the branches, looks down upon the wonderful God-man in amazement. At last the crowd comes to the tree. It looks as if Christ is going by, but He stops right under the tree, looks up, and says, "Zaccheus, make haste and come down."

I can imagine, the first thought in his mind was, "Who told Him my name? I was never introduced to Him." Ah! He knew him. Sinner, Christ knows all about you. He knows your name and your house. You need not try to hide from Him. He knows where you are, and all about you.

Some people do not believe in

SUDDEN CONVERSION

I should like them to answer me — when was Zaccheus converted? He was certainly in his sins when he went up into the tree; he certainly was converted when he came down. He must have been converted somewhere between the branch and the ground. It didn't take a long while to convert that publican! "Make haste and come down. I shall never pass this way again. This is my last visit." Zaccheus made haste and came down, and received Him joyfully. Did you ever hear of any one receiving Christ in any other way? He received Him joyfully. Christ brings joy with Him. Sin, gloom, and darkness flee away; light, peace and joy burst into the soul. Reader, may you come down from your high place, and receive Christ now.

Some one may ask, "How do you know that he was converted?" I think he gave very good evidence. I would like to see as fruitful evidence of conversion now-a-days. Let some rich men be converted, and give half their goods to feed the poor, and people will believe pretty quickly that it is genuine work! But there is better evidence even than that. "If I have taken anything from any man falsely, *I restore him fourfold.*" Very good evidence that. You say if people are converted suddenly, they won't hold out. Zaccheus held out long enough to restore fourfold. We should like to have a work that reaches men's pockets.

I can imagine one of his servants going to a neighbor next morning, with a check for $100, and handing it over. "What is this for?" "Oh, my master defrauded you out of $25 a few years ago, and this is restitution money." That would give confidence in Zaccheus' conversion! I wish a few cases like that would happen now, and then people would stop talking against sudden conversions.

The Lord goes to be the publican's guest, and while He is there the Pharisees began to murmur and complain. It would have been a good thing if Pharisees had died off with that generation; but, unfortunately, they have left a good many grandchildren, living down here in this nineteenth century, who are ever complaining, "This man receiveth *sinners.*" But while the Pharisees were complaining, the Lord uttered the words of text: "I did not come to Zaccheus to make him wretched, to condemn him, to torment him; I came to bless and save him. *The Son of Man is come to seek and to save that which was lost.*"

If there is a man or woman reading this who believes that he or she is *lost,* I have good news to tell you — Christ is come after you.

I was at the Fulton Street prayer meeting one Saturday night a good many years ago, and when the meeting was over, a man came to me, and said, "I would like to have you go down to the city prison tomorrow, and preach to the prisoners." I said I would be very glad to go. There was no chapel in connection with that prison, and I was to preach to them in their cells. I had to stand at a little iron railing and talk down a great, long, narrow passage way to some three or four hundred of them, I suppose, all out of sight. It was pretty difficult work; I never preached to bare walls before. When it was over I thought I would like to see to whom I had been preaching, and how they had received the gospel. I went to the first door, where the inmates could have heard me best, and looked in at a little window, and there were some men playing cards; I suppose they had been playing all the while. "How is it with you here?" I said. "Well, stranger, we don't want you to get a bad idea of us. False witnesses swore a lie, and that is how we are here." "Oh," I said, "Christ cannot save anybody here; there is nobody *lost.*" I went to the next cell. "Well, friend, how is it with you?" "Oh," said the prisoner, "the man that did the deed looked very much like me, so they caught me and I am here." He was innocent, too. I passed along to the next cell. "How is it with you?" "Well, we got into bad company, and the man that did it got clear, and we got taken up, but we never did anything." I went along to the next cell. "How is it with you?" "Our trial comes on next week, but they have nothing against us, and we'll get free." I went round nearly every cell, but the answer was always the same — they had never done anything. Why, I never saw so many innocent men together in my life! There was nobody to blame but the magistrates, according to their way of it. These men were wrapping their filthy rags of self-righteousness about them. And that has been the story for six thousand years.

I got discouraged as I went through the prison, on, and on, and on, cell after cell, and every man had an excuse. If he hadn't one, the devil helped him to make one.

I had got almost through the prison, when I came to a cell and found a man with his elbows on his knees, and his head in his hands. Two little streams of tears were running down his cheeks; they did not come by *drops* that time.

"What's the trouble?" I said. He looked up, the picture of remose and despair. "Oh, my sins are more than I can bear." "Thank God for that," I replied. "What," said he, "you are the man that has been preaching to us, ain't you?" "Yes." "I think you said you were a *friend?*" "I am." "And yet you are glad that my sins are more than I can bear!" "I will explain," I said; "if your sins are more than you can bear, won't you cast them on One who will bear them for you?" "Who's that?" "The Lord

Jesus." "He won't bear *my* sins." "Why not?" "I have sinned against Him all my life. "I don't care if you have; the blood of Jesus Christ, God's Son, cleanses from all sin." Then I told him how Christ had come to seek and save that which was lost; to open the prison doors and set the captives free. It was like a cup of refreshment to find a man who believed he was lost, so I stood there, and held up a crucified Savior to him. "Christ was delivered for our offences, died for our sins, rose again for our justification." For a long time the man could not believe that such a miserable wretch could be saved. He went on to enumerate his sins, and I told him that the blood of Christ could cover them all. After I had talked with him I said, "Now let us pray." He got down on his knees inside the cell, and I knelt outside. I said, "You pray." "Why," he said, "it would be blasphemy for me to call on God." "You call on God," I said. He knelt down, and, like the poor publican, he lifted up his voice and said, "God be merciful to me, a vile wretch!" I put my hand through the window, and as I shook hands with him a tear that burned down into my soul fell on my hand. It was a tear of repentance. He believed he was lost. Then I tried to get him to believe that Christ had come to save him. I left him still in darkness. "I will be at the hotel," I said, "between nine and ten o'clock, and I will pray for you." Next morning, I felt so much interested in him that I thought I must see him before I went back to Chicago. No sooner had my eye lighted on his face than I saw that remorse and despair had fled away. His countenance was beaming with celestial light; the tears of joy had come into his eyes, and the tears of despair were gone. The Sun of Righteousness had broken out across his path: his soul was leaping within him for joy; he had received Christ, as Zaccheus did, joyfully. "Tell me about it," I said. "Well, I do not know what time it was; I think it was about midnight. I had been in distress a long time, when all at once my great burden fell off, and now I believe I am the happiest man in New York." I think he was the happiest man

I saw from the time I left Chicago till I got back again. His face was lighted up with the light that comes from the celestial hills. I bade him good-bye, and I expect to meet him in another world.

Can you tell me why the Son of God came down to that prison that night, and, passing cell after cell, went to that one, and set the captive free? It was

BECAUSE THE MAN BELIEVED HE WAS LOST.

O that we would wake up to the thought of what it is to be lost! The world has been rocked to sleep by Satan, who is going up and down and telling people that it doesn't mean anything. I believe in the old-fashioned heaven and hell. Christ came down to save us from a terrible hell, and any man who is cast down to hell from here must go in the full blaze of the gospel, and over the mangled body of the Son of God.

We hear of a man who has lost his health, and we sympathize with him, and we say it is very sad. Our hearts are drawn out in sympathy. Here is another man who has lost his wealth, and we say, "That is very sad." Here is another man who has lost his reputation, his standing among men. "That is sadder still," you say. We know what it is to lose health and wealth and reputation, but what is the loss of all these things compared with the loss of the soul?

I was in an eye-infirmary in Chicago some time before the great fire. A mother brought a beautiful little babe to the doctor — a babe only a few months old, — and wanted the doctor to look at the child's eyes. He did so, and pronounced it blind — blind for life — it would never see again. The moment he said that, the mother seized it, pressed it to her bosom, and gave a terrible scream. It pierced my heart, and I could not but weep; the doctor wept; we could not help it. "Oh, my darling," she said, "are you never to see the mother that gave you birth? Oh, doctor, I cannot stand it. My child, my child!" It was a sight to move any heart. But what is the loss of eyesight to the loss of a soul? I had a thousand times rather have these eyes taken out of my head and go to the grave blind, than lose my soul. I have two sons and no one but God knows how I love them; but I would see their eyes dug out of their heads rather than see them grow up to manhood and go down to the grave without Christ and without hope. The loss of a soul! Christ knew what it meant. That is what brought Him from the bosom of the Father; that is what brought Him from the throne; that is what brought Him to Calvary. The Son of God was in earnest. When He died on Calvary it was to save a lost world; it was to save your soul and mine.

O the loss of the soul — how terrible it is! If you are still lost I beseech you do not rest until you have found peace in Christ. Fathers and mothers, if you have children out of the Ark, do not rest until they are brought into it. Do not discourage your children from coming to Christ. The Son of man came to save children as much as old grey haired men. He came for all, rich and poor, young and old. Young man, if you are lost may God show it to you, and may you press into the kingdom. The Son of man is come to seek and to save you.

There is a story told of Rowland Hill. He was once preaching in the open air to a vast audience. Lady Anne Erskine was riding by, and she asked who it was that was addressing the vast assembly. She was told that it was the celebrated Rowland Hill. Said she, "I have heard of him; drive me near the platform, that I may listen to him." The eye of Rowland Hill rested on her. He saw that she belonged to the aristocracy, and turning to some one, he inquired who she was. He went on preaching, and all at once he stopped. "My friends," he said, "I have got something here for sale." Everybody was startled to think that a minister was going to sell something in his sermon. "I am going to sell it by auction, and it is worth more than the crown of all Europe, it is the soul of Lady Anne Erskine. Will any one bid for her soul? Hark! methinks I hear a bid. Who bids? Satan bids. What will you give? I will give riches, honor, and pleasure; yea, I will give the whole world for her soul. Hark! I hear another bid for this soul. Who bids? The Lord Jesus Christ. Jesus, what will you give for this soul? I will give peace, and joy, and comfort that the world knows not of; yea, I will give eternal life for her soul." Turning to Lady Anne Erskine, he said, "You have heard the two bidders for your soul — which shall have it?" She ordered the footman to open the door, and pushing her way through the crowd, she said, "The Lord Jesus shall have my soul, if He will accept it."

That story may be true, or it may not; but there is one thing I *know* to be true — there are two bidders for your soul now. It is for you to decide which shall have it. Satan offers you what he cannot give; he is a liar, and has been from the foundation of the world. I pity the man who is living on the devil's promises. He lied to Adam, deceived him, stripped him of all he had, and then left him in his lost, ruined condition. And all the men since Adam, living on the devil's lies, the devil's promises, have been disappointed, and will be, down to the end of the chapter. But the Lord Jesus Christ is able to give all He offers, and He offers eternal life to every lost soul. The gift of God is eternal life. Who will have it? Will any one flash it over the wires, and let it go up to the throne of God, that you want to be saved?

Some time since a man told me he was anxious to be saved, but Christ had never sought for him. I said, "What are you waiting for?" "Why," he said, "I am waiting for Christ to call me. As soon as He calls me, I am coming." There may be others here who have got the same notion. Now I do not believe there is a man in this land that the Spirit of God has not striven with at some period of his life. I do not believe there is a person but Christ has sought after him. Bear in mind, He takes the place of the seeker. Every man who has ever been saved through these six thousand years was first sought after by God. No sooner did Adam fall, than God sought him. He had gone away frightened, and hid himself among the bushes in the garden, but God took the place of the seeker; and from that day to this God has always had the place of the seeker. No man or woman has ever been saved but that He sought them first.

What do we read in the fifteenth chapter of St. Luke? There is a shepherd bringing home his sheep into the fold. As they pass in, he stands and numbers them. I can see him counting one, two, three, up to ninety-nine. "But," says he, "I ought to have a hundred. I must have made a mistake"; and he counts them over again. "There are only ninety-nine here. I must have lost one." He does not say, "I will let him find his own way back." No! He takes the place of the seeker. He goes out into the móuntain, and hunts until he finds the lost one, and then he lays it on his shoulder and brings it home. Is it the sheep that finds the shepherd? No, it is the shepherd that finds and brings back the sheep. He rejoiced to find it. Undoubtedly the sheep was very glad to get back to the fold, but it was the shepherd who rejoiced, and who called his friends and said, "Rejoice with me."

Then there is that woman who lost the piece of money. Some one perhaps had paid her a bill that day, giving her ten pieces of silver. As she retires at night, she takes the money out of her pocket and counts it. "Why," she says, "I have only got nine pieces. I ought to have ten." She counts it over again. "Only nine pieces! Where have I been since I got that money? I am sure I have not been out of the house." She turns her pocket wrong side out, and there she finds a hole in it. Does she wait until the money gets back into her pocket? No. She takes a broom, and lights a candle, and sweeps diligently. She moves the sofa and the table and the chairs, and all the rest of the furniture, and sweeps in every corner until she finds it. And when she has found it, who rejoices? The piece of money? No;

the woman who finds it. In these parables, Christ brings out the great truth that God takes the place of seeker. People talk of finding Christ, but it is Christ who first finds them.

Another young man told me one night that he was too great a sinner to be saved. Why, they are the very men Christ came after. "This Man receiveth sinners and eateth with them." The only charge they could bring against Christ down here was that He was receiving bad men. They are the very kind He is willing to receive. All you have got to do is to prove that you are a sinner, and I will prove that you have got a Savior. And the greater the sinner, the greater need you have of a Savior. You say your heart is hard; well, then, of course, you want Christ to soften it. You cannot do it yourself. The harder your heart, the more need you have of Christ; the blacker you are, the more need you have of a Savior. If your sins rise up before you like a dark mountain, bear in mind that the blood of Jesus Christ cleanses from all sin. There is no sin so big, or so black, or so corrupt and vile, but the blood of Christ can cover it. So I preach the old gospel again, "The Son of Man is come to seek and to save that which was lost."

It was Adam's fall, his *loss,* that brought out God's love. God never told Adam, when He put him into Eden, that He loved him. It was his fall, his sin, that brought it out. A friend of mine from Manchester was in Chicago a few years ago, and he was very much interested in the city — a great city, with its 300,000 or 400,000 inhabitants, with its great railway centers, its lumber market, its pork market, and its grain market. He said he went back to Manchester and told his friends about Chicago. But he could not get anybody very much interested in it. It was a great many hundreds of miles away, and the people did not seem to care for hearing about it. But one day there came flashing along the wire the sad tidings that it was on fire; and, my friend said, the Manchester people became suddenly interested in Chicago! Every despatch that came they read. They bought up the papers, and devoured every particle of news. And at last, when the despatch came that Chicago was burning up, that 100,000 people were turned out of house and home, then every one became so interested that they began to weep for us. They came forward and laid down their money — some gave hundreds of dollars for the relief of the poor sufferers. It was the *calamity* of Chicago that brought out the love of Manchester, and of London, and of Liverpool. I was in that terrible fire, and I saw men that were wealthy stripped of all they had. That Sunday night, when they retired, they were the richest men in Chicago. Next morning they were paupers. I did not see a man weep. But when the news came flashing along the wire, "Liverpool gives ten thousand dollars; Manchester sends five thousand dollars; London is giving money to aid the city"; as the news kept flashing that help was coming, our city was broken hearted. I saw men weep then. The love that was shown us broke our hearts. So the love of God ought to break every heart to-day. It was love that brought Christ down here to die for us. It was love that made Him leave His place by the Father's throne and come down here *to seek and to save that which was lost.*

But now for the sake of these men who believe Christ never sought them, perhaps it would be well to say *how* He seeks. There are a great many ways in which He does so.

One night I found a man in the inquiry-room, and the Lord had been speaking to him by the prayers of a godly sister who died a little while ago. Her prayers were answered. He came into the inquiry-room trembling from head to foot. I talked to him about the plan of salvation, and the tears trickled down his cheeks, and at last he took Christ as his Savior. The Son of Man sought out that young man through the prayers of his sister, and then through her death.

Some of you have godly, praying mothers, who have prayed whole nights for your soul, and who have now gone to heaven. Did not you take their hand and promise that you would meet them there? That was the Son of God seeking you by your mother's prayers and your mother's death. Some of you have got faithful, godly ministers who weep for you in the pulpit, and plead with you to come to Christ. You have heard heart-searching sermons, and the truth has gone down deep into your heart, and tears have come down your cheeks. That was the Son of God seeking you. Some of you have had godly, praying Sabbath school teachers and superintendents, urging you to come to Christ. Some of you, perhaps, have got young men converted around you, and they have talked with you and pleaded with you to come to Christ. That was the Son of God seeking after your soul. Some of you have had a tract put into your hand with the startling title, "Eternity; Where will you spend it?" and the arrow has gone home. That was the Son of God seeking after you. Many of you have been laid on a bed of sickness, when you had time to think and meditate, and in the silent watches of the night, when everybody was asleep, the Spirit of God has come into your chamber, has come to your bedside, and the thought came stealing through your mind that you ought to be a child of God and an heir of heaven. That was the Son of God seeking after your lost soul. Some of you have had little children, and you have laid them in the cemetery. When that little child was dying you promised to love and serve God. Ah, have you kept your promise? That was the Son of God seeking you. He took that little child yonder to draw your affections heavenwards.

O friends, open the door of your heart and let the heavenly Visitor in. Do not turn Him away any longer. Do not say with Felix, "Go Thy way this time, and when I have a convenient season I will call for Thee." Make this a convenient season; make this the hour of your salvation. Receive the gift of God now, open the door of your heart, and say: "Welcome, thrice welcome into this heart of mine."

THE RESURRECTION

W e have for our subject, this morning, the Resurrection. The Resurrection is spoken of forty-two times in the New Testament. It is, you might say, one of the chief corner-stones in the religion of Jesus Christ. You might say that there are two principal truths taught all through the New Testament; the death, and resurrection, of Jesus Christ. You touch one, and you touch them both. In fact, you take that out of the New Testament, and you take out the key to the whole gospel of Jesus Christ.

Let me call your attention to what Christ said about his own resurrection. Matthew 16:21: "From that time forth began Jesus to show unto his disciples how that he must go unto Jerusalem, and suffer many things of the elders, and chief priests, and scribes, and be killed, and be raised again the third day." Then, while he was talking with his disciples after the transfiguration, we find in Matthew 17:9, that he said to the disciples, as they came down from the mountain: "Tell the vision to no man, until the Son of Man be risen again from the dead." Then in Mark 9:31: "For he taught his disciples and said unto them: The Son of man is delivered into the hands of men, and they shall kill him; and after that he is killed, he shall rise the third day."

Over and over again, he told the disciples that he was going to rise; and one very singular thing about it is that his enemies seemed to remember what he said about the resurrection, while his disciples seemed to have forgotten it; because, after he was dead, they went to Pilate and asked him to make the sepulchre secure, because they said, "While this deceiver was alive, he said he should rise again;" and we cannot find any place where the disciples remembered the words of the Lord Jesus that he should rise again. And when they laid him away Friday night, Joseph of Armathea and Nicodemus and those few women of Galilee followed him to his last resting place. There is not one solitary passage of Scripture that tells us that they had any hope of his resurrection. It seemed to have passed from their minds; or else they never received it when Christ told them, and he told them plainly.

In the 12th of Matthew we read that they wanted a sign: "Then certain of the Scribes and of the Pharisees answered, saying, Master, we would see a sign from thee. But he answered and said to them, An evil and adulterous generation seeketh after a sign, and there shall no sign be given to it but the sign of the prophet Jonah." And then he went on and told them that that should be the sign of his death and resurrection. Now, what was the sight? I was very much interested, some time ago, in hearing a Welchman tell me that he was preaching once on that subject of Jonah being the sign; and he said that he could just imagine when the news got to Nineveh about this man being sent from the Lord to Nineveh with this message, and how, when the captain got ashore, he reported about this man being on board, and at his own request being thrown overboard, and they saw the whale swallow Jonah; and, of course, Nineveh was greatly stirred up, at the idea of a man being sent from the Lord to Nineveh with a message, and being slain on the way because he had refused to go, and so had been swallowed up by the whale. There is death. But what must have been the stir in Nineveh when this very resurrected man came through the streets of Nineveh, preaching that they must repent or all perish. That was resurrection. And now Christ says that was the sign.

There are a great many people, even at this present time, who don't believe Christ has risen; they say his Spirit is still in the world, but his body never came up out of the grave. But then the Word of God teaches nothing of the kind. Earth and hell did all they could to keep that body in the grave; but they could not do it. He laid there Friday night, and all through the Jewish Sabbath; and his disciples were mourning and weeping. As I said before, they had given up all hope of ever seeing him again; but you can see those hands that were cold in death Friday night, and see Death hovering over the sepulchre, laughing and saying: "I hold my victim in my own embrace; he had to pay tribute to me. He said he was the resurrection and the life; and yet he has not escaped me." But the hour had come for Christ to conquer Death, for that was what he went into the grave for. Death didn't take him into the grave; he followed Death into his own dominion and took the whole territory and bound him hand and foot, and came up victorious, and brought up a few captives to show his mighty power.

——— Yes, my friend, Christ went down into the grave for you and me; and it seems to me that one of the most precious truths in the whole Word of God is that our Christ is not dead. He don't lay there in Joseph's sepulchre; but he is risen. And now just see the proof that we have of it. Men and angels, bear in mind, guarded that sepulchre; they were going to make sure that his body should not come up, that he should not rise; they had gone to Pilate and got him to put soldiers to watch the sepulchre, and they rolled a great stone over it and put the Roman seal on it, and there they had that body secure, perfectly safe. And early in the morning, we are told by the Evangelists, these same women started to go to the sepulchre to anoint his body, and found out that he was risen. Why, do you think if they had thought he was going to rise that they would have left that sepulchre? They would have lingered around it; it would have taken more than a hundred Roman soldiers to keep those disciples away from the sepulchre, if they thought he was going to rise. Now, early in the gray of the morning, you could see these women going toward the sepulchre. They had got their spices all ready to anoint that body again, and they were greatly troubled, because they did not know who was going to roll away the stone. And you see them as they draw near to the sepulchre; and the sun has just driven away the darkness of the night and that beautiful morning is bursting upon the earth, the best morning this world had ever seen. And one says to another, "Who shall roll away the stone?" But a messenger came from yon world of light; he flew faster than the morning light, and arrived first. And he rolled away the stone; and those men that had been sent there by Pilate, to watch and guard that sepulchre, began to tremble, and fell as dead men; they hadn't any power. One angel was enough to roll away that stone; not to let him out, but to let you and I look in to see that the sepulchre was empty, to let the morning light into that sepulchre to light it up that we might know that he had risen, "the first fruits of them that slept." Yes, thank God, he has conquered Death and the grave; and you can shout now, "O grave, where is thy victory!" He went down into the grave and conquered it, and came up out of it; and now he says, "Because I live, ye shall live also."

The news spread. These women soon found out that the sepulchre was empty, and they ran back and told the disciples; and Peter and John rushed off to the sepulchre and found that the body was not there. They lingered around the sepulchre, and then went home, saying, "It is no use; his enemies have got his body." And all the Roman government and all the leading men of the Jewish nation were opposed to these few weak disciples; and what could they do? Ah, there was one that loved him; she could not leave that empty sepulchre; she wanted to stay around, in the hope that she might get some news of what they had done with the body. While she was there, a man observed her and said, "Woman, why weepest thou?" And she said, "They have taken away my Lord, and I know not where they have laid him." And then he spoke to her, in that old familiar voice, and says, "Mary"; and she recognized him and said, "Rabboni, Master!" Oh, how her heart leaped within her for joy. He that was dead was alive! There was her Savior, standing right before her, and he said, "Go back and tell my brethren that I have risen." He had got on resurrection ground, and he could call them "brethren," and put them on a level with himself.

What joyful news for her to take; what a blessed privilege to go and bear the tidings of the resurrection, the first one that got the blessed news. He out of that very one cast out seven devils, and now she was to take the tidings back to Jerusalem that the Lord had risen. She had seen him with her own eyes; he had spoken to her; it was a living body; it was not his spirit, but his own body that had come out of that sepulchre, although the disciples would not believe it. And while she was spreading the news, some others took it up to spread the story; and all at once Christ stood before them. That was his second appearing; and he told John to tell them to go back to Jerusalem and tell that he had risen. And I think if you would look through your Bibles carefully, you will find that ten different times he appeared to his disciples, not in the Spirit, but in the body, in person. I want to get this thing established in all our minds, that Christ has come out of the grave personally, that his body has gone back to haven. The same body they crucified; the same body they laid in Joseph's sepulchre has come out of the jaws of death and out of the sepulchre; and he has passed through the heavens and gone back on high. We are told he had an interview with Peter, who is alluded to as Simon and as Cephas. We can imagine what took place at that interview, and that Peter's old difficulty was settled. Peter denied him, but at that interview Christ forgave him. What a Sabbath it must have been for Peter! What a blessed day for that poor backslider! And if there is some backslider here to-day, who will have an interview with the Son of God, he will forgive you this Easter morning, and blot out all your wanderings and all your sins, if you will come back; and it will be a joyful day for you.

Late in the afternoon, that same day, Jesus appeared to the two men who were walking back to Emmaus, a village about eight miles from Jerusalem; and they constrained him to go in and take tea with them. After he vanished from their sight, they walked back to Jerusalem, and told the joyful news to the disciples that the Lord had risen; but Thomas was absent on that occasion. And while they were telling the good news, Jesus stood in their midst. They turned pale; and he said, "Don't be frightened. It is me, only me. Put your finger in these wounds that were made on Calvary; thrust your hand in my side if you like; it is only me; it is not a spirit." He wanted those men to be convinced that the body had come up out of the grave. He asked for something to eat, and they gave him some fish; and he ate before them and said, "Peace be unto you," and breathed on them the Holy Ghost, and said "Receive ye the Holy Ghost." That makes five times that he appeared to the disciples when he arose that blessed Easter Sunday.

Now Thomas was absent, and the news soon reached him, but he would not believe what was told him. When the next Lord's day came the eleven were assembled in that room, with the windows fastened and the doors bolted, the Lord stood there again; and he spoke to Thomas, and he told him to put his finger into the wounds, and to thrust his hand into his side; and Thomas cried out, "My Lord and my God." He didn't have to put his hand there; he knew it; he heard his voice; his infidelity and unbelief was scattered to the four winds; he believed then and there. And then the Lord said, "Blessed are those that have not seen, but yet believe." He pronounced a benediction upon you and I here, if we will only believe on him. "Blessed are those that have not seen, but yet believe."

The next time we hear of Christ, he appears to John and

James and Peter and Nathaniel, and two other disciples, while fishing. They were out all night and had caught nothing; and about daybreak there was a man seen on shore, and he said, "Children, have you any meat?" "No, we haven't got anything." He told them to cast the net on the right side, and they got a haul of 143 large fishes and the net didn't break. And John said, "Peter, that is the Lord;" they knew him. Success is always with those the Lord is with. They cast that net at his word; they knew it was his power, and Peter was so anxious to get to him — ah, Peter loved the Lord, if he did deny him once — that he leaped right into the water and swam ashore, and got there first to meet him. And he had a fire made, and they had some bread, and took a resurrection breakfast.

Oh, may every one hear his voice this morning, saying, "Come and eat;" and then we can go out and feed others! I hope every Christian this morning will get some food.

And then Paul tells us, over in Corinthians, that he appeared to over five hundred at one time; but where it took place, we don't know. It is supposed by a great many to have been over in one of the mountains of Galilee; and he talked with them, and it might have been at that time that he told them to "Go and preach the gospel to every creature;" and carry the tidings around the world. "Lo, I am with you, I will not leave you; if I go away I will send the Holy Ghost to comfort you, and greater works he shall do." Some one says a good many reformations die out with the reformer; but this reformer has gone upon high, to carry out his own reformation. He is at the right hand of God; and where can he be to carry on his work any better than up yonder? We are told by Paul that he appeared once to James; but we have no glimpse of that interview.

The last interview he had with them was in Jerusalem; and he took the little band of believers out of the city, down through the Eastern gate, down through the valley of Jehosaphat, over the brook Kedron, past that garden where he sweated drops of blood, past Calvary, over the brow of the hill, and went out past Bethany, where Martha and Mary and Lazarus (the resurrected man) lived; and perhaps right there, under a cluster of little olive trees, he met his disciples for the last time to bid them farewell, and gave them his parting message. Now he says: "I go home; I go back to the throne (he had been out of the grave forty days); now I ascend to God." And while he was blessing them — for you know he came blessing, the first thing he said on that memorable mountain when he preached that wonderful sermon, there were nine blessings right out of his heart, he could not go on until he got them out: "Blessed are the poor"; Blessed are the peacemakers"; Blessed, blessed; and he recited those wondrous things and blessed them. And while he was blessing them, he began to ascend; and he rose higher and higher; and his voice grew fainter and fainter, and at last it died away in the clouds; and the clouds received him out of their sight.

I can imagine up in the clouds there was a chariot from the throne, to take him back home; his work was finished; he rides like Elijah in that golden chariot, and sweeps away through the heavens to the throne. Look at him on his way to that world where all honor him, and all love him! And as he went sweeping upon his way home, he did not forget his little church; he could see them, but they could not see him; and I can see Peter and John looking up, in hopes that there will be a break in the clouds so that they may see him once more. And while they stand there, gazing up into heaven, you can see tears trickling down their cheeks, their hearts have almost gone out of their body; and he looks back and sees them; and he says to two of the angels who were conveying him home, "Go back, and tell those men that I will come back again." I don't know but they were the two Mary saw in the sepulcre; and they said: "Ye men of Gallilee, why stand ye gazing up into heaven? This same Jesus which is taken up from you into heaven, shall so come in like manner as ye have seen him go into heaven." Thank God, he is coming back! It is only a question of time. And in such a day and hour as we think not, he will render the heavens and come back. Lift up your hearts, for the time of your redemption draweth near. We don't worship a dead Savior! He has passed through the heavens, gone up on high, led captivity captive and taken his seat at the right hand of God.

Paul saw him, and Stephen saw him, standing at the right of God. He is there, my friends. Thanks be to God, he is not here. They laid him in Joseph's sepulchre; he is risen and up yonder, and, not only that, "If I go, I will send the Holy Ghost." And after he had been gone ten days, the Holy Ghost came, and just fulfilled his word. Do you think this audience would have been here this morning, if it had not been for the Holy Ghost? Do you believe preaching the gospel for 1800 years would have kept the people, if it had not have been for the Holy Ghost coming? Ah, my friends, it is the Holy Ghost he sent when he went into heaven. And now, my friends, let me say, in closing, if we will just preach more about the resurrected Savior, and if we live more about him and try and realize the power that we get in him and through him, we will accomplish more this last month of our labors than we have accomplished in all the rest of our lives.

Oh, may God help us to realize what a precious truth we have to preach; that we are not worshiping a dead Savior; that he is a resurrected Savior, and in such a day and hour as we think not he will return. And although we do not know when that will be, there is one thing we do know, and that is that he has promised to come; and that day is not far distant; we haven't but a little while to work. As Christine Evans says: "The songs of these bursting sepulchres, when Christ shall come, will be sweeter than the song of the morning star." We shall come up from the grave, by and by, with a shout. "He is the first fruits;" he has gone into the vale, and will call us by and by. The voice of the Son of God shall wake up the slumbering dead! Jacob will leave his lameness, and Paul will leave his thorn in the flesh; and we shall come up resurrected bodies, and be forever with the Lord. I pity those people who know nothing about the resurrection of Christ, and think Christ does not live, and was merely a man, and perished in the grave of Joseph of Arimathea. What hope have they got?

Oh, what gloom and darkness settles down upon this world, if it was not for the glorious day of resurrection. And those that have been sown in dishonor and corruption shall be raised, by and by, in glory and honor; they shall come up out of their graves, and we shall be forever with them. Oh, may this blessed truth take hold of all our hearts, and may we go out from this Tabernacle and spread the news that the Lord has risen. He has gone up on high, and he will bless the sons of men, if they will receive a blessing from him.

BLESSED HOPE

I HAVE selected for my subject this afternoon the blessed hope. We are told to be ready to give a reason for the hope we have within us, and what we want to do is to find out what our hope is. I believe there are a great many people that are hoping and hoping, when they have no ground for hope. I don't know of any better way to find out whether we have true ground for the hope we have within us than to look in Scripture to see what the Scripture has to say.

Now, faith is one thing, and hope is another. When hope takes the place of faith, it is a snare. Faith is to work and trust. Some one has said that life is to enjoy and obey and be like God; but hope is to wait and trust; to wait and expect; in other words, that hope is the daughter of faith. I heard a very godly man once say that joy was like the larks, that sang in the morning when it was light, but hope was like the nightingale, that sang in the dark; so that hope was really better than joy.

Most anyone can sing in the morning when everything is bright, and everything going well; but hope sings in the dark, in the mist and the fog, looks through all the mist and darkness into the clear day. Faith lays hold of what is in the Scripture, faith is laying hold of that which is within the veil, and what is in heaven for us.

Now, we cannot get on any better without hope than we can without faith. The farmer who sows his seed, sows it in the hope of a harvest; the merchant buys his goods in the hope to find customers, and the student toils in the hope that he will reap by-and-by.

Now, I want to call your attention to the three classes of people that are gathered here to-day. They are those that have no hope, those that have a false hope, and those that have a good hope. I do not know that there is any one here to-day that would come under the first head. It is pretty hard to find any one in this world that has not some hope. Once in a while you will come across a person that has no hope in this life or the life to come. It is from that class that our suicides come. When men or women get to that point that they have no hope in this life, they become utterly discouraged, cast down, no hope in the life to come, believe when they die that is the last of them, atheists in their views, believe there is no hereafter, they put an end to their existence.

The point I want to call your attention to in the class that has no earthly hope, is this, "A child is sick; a doctor is called, and he looks at the child and says there is no hope; but the moment the mother loses hope of the child living in this world another hope comes up; she hopes to see the child again in another world. Hope comes and cheers that mother in trouble.

When Mr. Curtin was governor of Pennsylvania, a young man in that state was convicted of murder and was sentenced to be hung. His friends tried in every way they could to get him released. The young man was holding on to a hope that he would be released; they could not make him believe that he had to die. At last the governor sent for George H. Stuart, and said to him, "I wish you would go down to that jail and tell that young man there is no hope; tell him that there is not one ray of hope; that on the day appointed he must die; that I am not going to pardon him." Mr. Stuart said when he went into the jail the young man's countenance lit up, and he says, "Ah, I am sure you brought me good news. What does it say?" Mr. Stuart said he would never be the bearer of such a message again. He said that he lay down beside him on the iron bed, and said, "My friend, I am sorry to tell you there is not any hope. The governor says you must die at the appointed time. He will not pardon you. He sent me down here to take away this false hope you have got, and to tell you you have to die." He said the young man fainted away, and it was some time before they could bring him to. The poor man's heart was broken. He had been holding on to a false hope. In that case, that young man was not without hope, because he could repent, for God does forgive murderers, and become a child of God; become a saved man. Hope comes right in there. Even these men that think that they have no hope, there is hope for them if they will only turn to the God of hope, and to the God of the Bible.

That is only one class. Job speaks about days passing without hope; but then he does not mean that there was not any hope beyond this life, because Job says in another place, "I know my Redeemer liveth, and that I shall see Him." He was like Paul. He knew in whom he believed. He had a hope in the darkness and fog; when those waves of persecution came dashing up against him, and in the midst of the storm and conflict you could hear Job cry out, "I know my Redeemer liveth." He had a hope. So I say it is hard to find any one that comes under the first head. Most people have some sort of hope.

Now I come to the second head, people that have a false hope. I contend that a man or woman that is resting in false hope is really worse off than one who has no hope in this world; because if a man wakes up to the fact that he has no hope, there is a chance of rousing him to seek a hope that is worth having. The moment you begin to talk with these men that have a false hope, they run right off into their fortress and say, "I am all right; I have got a hope." You can hardly find a man or woman in all this city to-day that has not a hope. But how many are resting in a false hope, a miserable, treacherous hope that is good for nothing? You can't find a drunkard that has not a hope. He hangs on to the rumbottle with one hand and hope with the other; but his hope is a miserable lie; it is a refuge of lies that he has hid behind. You can't find a harlot that walks the streets of this city but that has some hope. You can hardly find a thief but that has some hope.

Now, what we want to do is to examine ourselves, and see whether we have a hope that will stand the test of the judgment. We want to know whether we have a true hope or a false hope. If it is a false hope, the quicker we find it out the better. We don't want to be resting in a false hope. That has caused nearly all the mischief we have had in this country during the past few years. All these defaulters have come from that class. They were trusting in a false hope. They said, "I will take a little from the bank or from my employer. I will just overdraw my account a few thousand dollars, but I will replace it." But they went on drawing out, and drawing out, and this false hope kept saying, "I can make it all right in a few days." They were led on and on by false hope until at last they got beyond hope, and could not pay it back. They were ruined. They were not only ruined—it would be a good thing if they stopped there, but look at their wives and their children and their relatives, their parents and their loved ones that they have ruined. They didn't intend to become ruined men. They didn't intend to bring a blight upon their families and upon their prospects here. A false hope led them on step by step.

Now, my friends, let us be honest with ourselves to-day, and ask ourselves honestly before God and man, "What is my hope?" Well, there is a lady up there in the gallery says, "I joined the Methodist church ten years ago." Very well, suppose you did, what is your hope to-day? "Well, my hope is all right; I joined the church." But that is not going to stand the light of eternity. It don't say that you have got to join some church. A man or woman may belong to a church and have not the spirit of Jesus Christ.

Yes, and another one says over there, "I have a better hope than that; I belong to the Congregational church, and go out to all the meetings." A person may go to all the meetings and not have a true hope. Do you know that? If you allow the meetings to take the place of Jesus Christ, and let the church come in the denomination that you belong to, and take the place of Jesus Christ, you are resting on a rotten foundation, and you are building your house on a sandy foundation, and when the storms come, the house will fall. There is nothing but Jesus Christ that will do. But these false hopes will be swept away by-and-by. God's hail will sweep away the refuges of lies. It says in the eleventh chapter of Proverbs and seventh verse, "The hope of the unrighteous man perisheth." Now, if I belong to the church and am unrighteous, I may have a hope, but that is going to perish, and it may be I will not find it out until it is too late to get a good hope. It is a good deal better to find it out here to-day, when I have a chance to repent of my sin, and turn to God and get a true hope, than it is to go with my eyes closed in the delusion that I am coming out all right.

There is another passage here, in Job, twenty-seventh chapter and eighth verse, "For what is the hope of the hypocrite, though he hath gained, when God taketh away his soul? What is his hope good for? The hope of the hypocrite is not good for anything. A man may gain by his hypocrisy; a man may put on the garb of religion, and profess to be what he is not, and may gain by it; there is no doubt of that; some do that, and they gain a little; but what shall it profit a man if he does gain by his hypocrisy, and God taketh away his soul? His hope is gone. It was a treacherous hope. It was good for nothing.

"But then," you may say, "I am not an unrighteous man; I don't come under that head at all, and I am no hypocrite." Well, I am afraid a good many of us that think we are not hypocrites are more or less hypocrites after all. The trouble is, men are trying to pass themselves off for more than they are worth. They are trying to make people believe they are better than they really are. God wants honesty. God wants downright uprightness, if you will allow me the expression. He wants us to be truthful and upright in all our transactions. If we are not, our profession don't help us. You may belong to this church or to that church. You may say your prayers, and you may go through the form of religion, but it will not help you. What is the hope of the hypocrite when God shall take away his soul? Suppose he has gained by his hypocrisy, there is not a thing, I believe, that God detests more than He does hypocrisy. He detests that sin more than He does all others. Jesus tore away the false hope of some of His disciples and told them, "Except your righteousness exceed the righteousness of the Scribes and Pharisees, ye shall in no wise enter into the kingdom of God." Ah, there will be many a man and many a woman, I am afraid, by-and-by, who will wake up and find their hope has been a false one after all.

Then there is another hope that is false. Men say, "I think God is very merciful, and that it will come out all right in the end." God has declared with an oath that He will not clear the guilty. What folly it is for a man to stand up and say, "I know I swear now and then; but then God don't mean anything when He says I shan't swear. God is only winking at sin. It will come out all right. The blasphemer, the drunkard, the libertine, and the man who is vile and polluted in heart will be just the same at the end of the route. That is my hope." Well, it is a false hope. If there is a drunkard here to-day, let me tell you that your hope is perfectly worthless, because God says that no drunkard shall inherit the kingdom of heaven. That we find not only in the Old Testament, but in the New. And if there is a man here that sells liquor, that is party to the hellish act of putting the bottle in his neighbor's hand, there is not any hope for him. I don't care how much money you give to help build your churches. I don't care if you have the best pew in one of your large churches, and walk down the broad aisle every Sunday with your wife and children, and take your seat there. "Woe be to the man that putteth the bottle to his neighbor's lips." God has pronounced a curse against that man. Things look altogether different when we stand before the judge of all the earth.

Yes, but then there is another man. He says, "I can go on as I am, and by-and-by when I am sick, I can repent on my death-bed." I think that is a false hope. And let me say, I think there is any quantity of lying in the sick-room, a good many false hopes held out to the sick. Here is a person dying, and the doctor comes in, and he knows very well that the disease is fatal, and knows that person can't live ten days, and he says, "I think you will be well and out in a few days, in the course of thirty days." He knows very well it is death. They say to these consumptives when they see that awful look in the face; when they see his form is wasting, they say, "Well, I think you will be out again in the spring; when the flowers begin to blossom, and nature begins to unfold itself, you will be out again," when they know it is downright lying. O, the false hopes that are held out to sick and the dying! Then at the funeral people will stand up and pronounce a eulogy over a a man that died in his sins when there is not a chance for his soul. God says, "The soul that sinneth it shall die. He has not sought eternal life. He has spurned the gift of God and trampled the Bible under his feet. Look at the lying at funerals; false hopes that are held out. What God wants is to have us real, as He is real, and if our hope is not a hope that will stand the test of eternity, then the quicker we find it out the better.

Then there is another false hope, which I think is worse, perhaps, than any other, and that is that a man can repent beyond the grave. There is a class of people who say, "I can go on in my sins and live as I am living, and I can repent beyond the grave." Now, if there is a chance for a man to repent beyond the grave, I can't find it between the lids of the Bible. I believe that if a man dies in his sin he is banished from God, and I believe that when Jesus Christ said, "If ye die in your sins, where I am ye cannot come," he meant what he said.

So, if our hope is false, let us find it out to-day. Let us be honest with ourselves, and ask God to show it to us. If our hope is not on the solid rock, if we are building our house on the sand, let us find it out. You may say, "My hope is as good as yours. My house is as good-looking house as yours." That may be. It might be a better looking house than mine. But the important thing is the foundation. What we want is to be sure that we have a good foundation. A man may build up a very good character, but he may not have it on a good foundation. If he is building a house on the sand, when storm and trials come, down will come all his hopes. A false hope is worse than no hope. If you have a false hope to-day, make up your mind that you will not rest until you reach a hope that is worth having.

Now, here is a test that I think we can put to ourselves. If we have got the spirit of Jesus Christ, our life will be like His; that is, we will be humble, loving. We will not be jealous, will not be ambitious, self-seeking, covetous, revengeful, but we will be meek, tender-hearted, affectionate, loving, kind and Christ-like, and we will be all the time growing in those graces. Now, we can tell whether we have that spirit or not. "If any one have not the spirit of Christ, he is none of His." Now, that is a sign that we have a good hope, and if we haven't got the spirit of Christ, our hope is worthless.

Now, I was speaking about that house on the foundation. If you will turn to Isaiah, twenty-eighth chapter and sixteenth verse, you will find that the foundation is already laid. "Therefore; thus saith the Lord God. Behold, I lay in Zion for a foundation a stone, a tried stone, a precious corner stone, a sure foundation;

he that believeth shall not make haste." There it is tried; it is a precious corner stone; it is a sure foundation. It was tried when Christ was here. He is the chief corner stone. He was tried. The Scribes tried Him. The Sadducees tried Him. He was tried by the law. He kept the law. He was tried by, and He overcame death. He was tried by Satan. Satan came and presented temptation after temptation, and He said, "Get thee hence." He overcame Satan. He was tried by the grave, and He conquered the grave. This stone has been tested and tried. Now, if we build on that, we have a sure foundation. There is none other name under heaven given among men whereby we must be saved. "There is no other foundation that man can lay than that is laid," and all that build on that foundation shall be saved. Let the storms come then and try that foundation. It has been tried. Your foundation, if you build on any other, has never been tested. It has not been tried. Your hope has not been tried. Our hope has, because our hope is in Jesus Christ, and it was put to the test, and we have got a hope that is sure and firm, if we are in Christ. Now, a false hope just flatters people. It is a great flatterer. It makes people think they are all right when they are all wrong. Some one has said that false hopes are like spider webs. The maid comes in with a broom and sweeps them all down. When a storm comes, the foundation of our false hopes is all gone. Suppose death should come and look you in the face this afternoon, and say to you, "This is your last day," and should begin to lay his cold, icy hand upon you, and you should begin to look around to see if you had got a foundation and a good hope. Would you be ready to meet God? That is the question. Now, what may happen any day let us be ready for every day. You know very well there is not one of us but that may be summoned this very day into the presence of God. Have you got a hope that will stand the dying hour? Have you got a hope that will stand the test? If you have not, you can give up your false hope to-day and get a good one, a hope that is worth having, that has been tried and tested.

There were two millers that used to take care of a mill, and —— every night at midnight the miller used to get into his boat from his house, and go down the stream to the mill; used to get out about two or three hundred yards above the dam, and go to the mill. His brother miller would take the boat and row back to the house. One night this miller went down as usual at midnight and fell asleep, and when he woke up found he was almost going over the dam, the water going over the dam having waked him. He realized in a moment his condition, that if he went over that dam it was sure death, and he seized the oars and tried to row back, but the current was too strong, and he could not pull against it, but he managed in the darkness to get his boat near the shore, and he caught hold of a little twig. He went to pull himself out of the boat, and the twig began to give way at the roots. He looked all around, and could find nothing else to get hold of; but he could just hold on to the twig and keep his boat from going over the dam. If he pulled a little harder and tried to pull himself up, the little twig would give way; and he just cried then for help. His hope was not `a good one. He would perish if he let go, and perish if he held on. He just cried at the top of his voice for help, and help came. They came and threw a rope over the cleft of the rock, and he let go of the twig and laid hold of the rope, and was saved.

I have come here to throw a rope over to you, and to give you a good hope. Now, we have a hope here that is worth having. Let that false hope of yours go; you will perish if you will hold on to it. Let it go and lay hold of a hope that is set before you.

Now, you know that hope in Scripture never is used to express a doubt. When people say they hope they are Christians, it is not really proper. You cannot find any Christians in the Bible who say they hope they are Christians. It is something that has already taken place. We don't hope we are Christians. If a man asks me if I am a married man, I would not say I hope I am. That would cast a reflection on my marriage vows. If a man asks me if I am an American, I would not say I hope I am. I was born in this country. I am an American. I am not anything else. Now, if I have been born of God, born of the spirit, and I contend it is our privilege to know, I don't say, "I hope I am a Christian." I know in Whom I have believed. I will tell you what hope is used for in Scripture. It is used to express our hope of the resurrection, or the coming of the Lord Jesus Christ, something to take place. It is a sure hope. About every time that hope is used in Scripture, it is used either to express our hope of the resurrection, or the coming back of our Lord and Master. That is the blessed hope in Titus. We are waiting for our Lord and Master from heaven. We have not a doubt. It is a sure hope. And yet a great many people seem to think that hope here in the Bible is used to express a doubt. "We hope that we are Christians." We ought to know that we are His. We ought to know that we have passed from death unto life. We ought to know in Whom we have believed, that we are looking forward to the time when these vile bodies shall be raised incorruptible; when that which has been sown in weakness shall be raised with power. We are living in the glorious hope that when our dead shall come back again, the loved ones that are laid away in the cemeteries shall come when the Lord of heaven shall descend with a shout. "When the trump of God is heard, the dead in Christ shall rise first; then we which are alive and remain shall be caught up, together with them in the clouds, to meet the Lord in the air."

So we stand with our loins girded and our lights burning, waiting for the coming of the Master.

Now, it says here in Proverbs, "The hope of the righteous shall be gladness." "Happy is he that hath the God of Jacob for his hope, whose hope is in the Lord." It is not in some resolution that he has made; it is not in some act of his; it is not that he has joined some church; it is not that he reads his Bible, or that he says his prayers. His expectation is from God; his hope is in God. Never was a man disappointed who put his hope in God. God will fulfill His word. There is no such thing as a man being disappointed that puts his hope in God. But the trouble is, you know, we are putting our hopes in one another, and we are being disappointed. We are putting our hopes in ourselves, and our treacherous hearts are disappointing us, and then we are cast down. But what we want is to put our hope in Him, not ourselves. A well-grounded hope is good for all time. It is good in poverty. It is good in sickness. It is good in the dying hour; and when we lay a body down in the grave, we have a hope in its coming back again. We lay down with sure hope, a glorious hope. O, how hope cheers us! You know it was Hopeful (in Bunyan's *Pilgrim's Progress*) that came along and cheered Christian. That is what hope is for. We are looking forward to a blessed hope.

Now, there is a passage in the sixth chapter of Hebrews that I want to call your attention to, "That by two immutable things, in which it was impossible for God to lie, we might have a strong consolation, who had fled for refuge to lay hold upon the hope set before us; which hope we have as an anchor to the soul, both sure and steadfast, and which enters into that within the veil; whither the forerunner is for us entered, even Jesus, made an high priest forever after the order of Melchisedec." What the anchor is to the ship, hope is to the soul; as long as the anchor holds, the ship is perfectly safe.

Now, if I were to die this afternoon, and were to give a reason for the hope that is within me, I will tell you where I would find it; not in my feelings, not in my resolutions, not that I joined the church twenty odd years ago. I believe it is all right to unite with the church, and work for it. We ought to love the church; it is the dearest institution on earth. If I was going to die this afternoon, my faith would be right here, "Verily,

verily, I say unto you, he that heareth my word, and believeth on Him that sent me, hath everlasting life, and shall not come into condemnation, but is passed from death unto life." Now, if I did not get eternal life by believing on the Lord Jesus Christ when I came to Him, what did I get? If eternal life is not the gift of God, what is it? Then, if we have eternal life, we have something that cannot perish. It is a life that carries me beyond the grave; that reaches away over on to resurrection ground; that carries me on and on forever. The wages of sin is death, but the gift of God is eternal life. Eternal life is a gift, and I just took it. That is my hope. I don't want any other hope. If I had to die to-day, I could just pillow my dying head upon the truth of that verse, and rest it there.

A man said to me the other day, "How do you feel?" I said, "It has been so long since I have thought of myself, I don't know; I would have to stop to think it over."

I thank God my salvation don't rest upon my feelings. I thank God my hope is not centered in my feelings. If it was, it would be a very treacherous thing. I would be very hopeful one day and cast down the next day. I would not give much for a hope that is anchored in my feelings. I would not give much for a hope that is based upon my treacherous heart. But I tell you that a hope that is based upon Jesus Christ's word is a hope worth having. Now, he said it; let us believe it; let us lay hold of it by faith. "Verily, verily," which means "truly, truly," "he that heareth my word"—I have heard it. Satan can't make me believe that I have not. I have read it; I have handled it—"He that heareth my word and believeth on Him that sent Me hath everlasting life." It don't say that you shall have it when you come to die, but hath it right here this afternoon, before you go out of this church. That is a hope worth having, isn't it? "Hath everlasting life, and shall not come into condemnation," which means "into judgment," but "is passed from death unto life." There is my hope. I have stood there for twenty odd years.

I have been assailed by doubts. I have been assailed by unbelief. I have been attacked by the enemy of all righteousness; but I tell you for twenty odd years I have been able to stand fair and square right on that rock. God said it. I believe it; God said it. I lay hold of it, and I just rest right there. What we want is to let our hope go down like an anchor into the word of God, and that gives us something to rest upon.

A great many people are waiting for some feeling. I will venture to say that more than half of this audience have come here to-day, and taken their seats in the hope that something will be said that shall impress them. You say, "I hope that man will say something that will impress me." You are waiting for some impression, something to strike you. There is a man up in my native town, now fifty-eight years old, with whom I have talked I don't know how many times, and every time I talk to him he says, "Well, it hasn't struck me yet." "What do you mean?" "Well," he says, "it hasn't struck me yet." "Well," I said, "that is a queer expression. What do you mean?" He would come out to meetings, and wait through the meeting for something to strike him. "What do you mean?" "Well, I say it hasn't struck me yet." You laugh at it, but that is yourself. You need not laugh at yourself. You will find the church is full of people who are waiting for something to strike them. What we want is to take God's word, and let the feelings take care of themselves. God said it. I will believe it, and I will rest my soul upon the word of God, not upon my feelings. Just take another word, "He came unto His own, and His own received Him not; but to as many as received Him, to them gave He power to become the sons of God, even to them that believe on His name." To as many as received Him. It is not dogma; it is not creed; it is not doctrine; it is not feeling; it is not an impression; but it is a person. "As many as received *Him,* to them gave He power to become the sons of God." We get power to serve God, power to live for God, power to work for God by receiving Christ, and there is no power until we do receive Him. What we want is to receive God's gift to the world. When He gave up Christ, He gave all He had. He literally emptied heaven. And He wants you to take Christ as you would take any other gift and receive it. Lay hold of that gift, and it will give you hope, and if you should, inside of twenty-four hours you can say, "The anchor holds; I have a hope." If God said if I would receive His Son, He would give me power to receive Him. I trust Him, and that is all He asks us to do. Let not any one here to-day say he can't believe on the Lord Jesus Christ. You have the power if you will. The will is the key to the human heart. "Ye will not come unto Me that ye might have life." Ye will not come unto Me and get this good hope. You can have it. Take it. God offers it to you. You can lay hold of this hope to-day. You can become His if you will.

THE THIEF ON THE CROSS

*And he said unto Jesus, Lord remember me when thou comest
into thy kingdom.* — Luke 23:42

Every one who is not a Christian ought to be interested in
this man, to know how he was converted. Any man who objects
to sudden conversions should give attention to how this man
was converted. If conversions are gradual, this poor thief could
not have been converted. If a man, who has lived a good, consistent life cannot be suddenly converted, then this thief didn't
have any chance. If it takes six months, six weeks, or six days
to convert a man, there was no chance for this thief. Turn to
the 23d chapter of Luke, and you will see how the Lord dealt
with this man, who was not only a thief, but the worst kind of
a thief. It was only the worst classes who were condemned to
die the death upon the cross. We find this man was condemned
to that most ignominious death.

When a prominent man dies, we are anxious to get his last
words and acts. We ask, What did he do? What were his last
words and acts? The last act of the Son of God was to save a
sinner. He commenced his ministry by saving sinners, and ended
it by saving this poor thief. "Shall the prey be taken from the
mighty, or the lawful captive delivered? But thus saith the Lord:
Even the captives of the mighty shall be taken away, and the
prey of the terrible shall be delivered." He took this captive from
the jaws of death. He was on the borders of hell, and Christ
snatched him from the grasp of Satan. We are told by Matthew

and Mark that these thieves came to curse; they both reviled Christ. They were not only thieves but revilers; and they cast it into his teeth that he said, "I am the Son of God." Here, then, our Lord is condemned by them. There were none to pity them. Perhaps they might have had some mother in the crowd, but no one else had any pity for them. Justice cried out: "Let them be put to death; they are not worthy to live."

The question is: What was it converted one of these thieves? I do not know, but I have an idea that it was Christ's prayer. When Christ cried on the cross: "Forgive them, for they know not what they do!" I can imagine that did what the scourge did not do. They had gone through the trial, and their hearts had not been broken; they had been nailed to the cross, but their hearts had not been subdued; they raised no cry to God for mercy, but they reviled the Son of God. But when they heard the cry: "Father, forgive them, for they know not what they do!" one of them says: "That man is not of the same spirit as we are. I could call out the thunderbolts of heaven to consume them." There they are crying, "Save thyself if thou be the Son of God;" yet they are crying this, the Son of God is crying to his Father to have mercy on them. It flashed into his soul that this was the Son of God, and that moment he confessed his sin. He turned to the other thief and rebuked him, and says, "Dost thou not fear God?" The fear of God fell upon him. There is not much hope of a man's being saved until the fear of God comes upon him. Solomon says, "The fear of God is the beginning of wisdom." We read in Acts that great fear fell upon the people: that was the fear of the Lord. That was the first sign that conviction had entered the soul of the thief. "Dost thou not fear God?" That was the first sign we have of life in that condemned man.

The next thing, he justifies Christ: "He hath done nothing amiss." When men are talking against Christ, they are a great way from becoming Christians. Now he says, "He hath done nothing amiss." There was the world mocking him; but right there, in the midst of thieves, you can hear that thief crying out, "This man hath done nothing amiss." "But," he says, "we are suffering justly." Now he took his place among the sinners, instead of trying to justify himself. He says: "We suffer justly; we have done wrong, and our condemnation is just." There is no hope for a sinner until he admits that his condemnation is just. The great trouble is, people are trying to make out they are not sinners; and therefore there is no chance of reaching them. But this thief said, "Our sentence is just;" and he took his place among sinners. There is no hope for a sinner until he sees the condemnation is a just condemnation; because he has sinned, and come short of the glory of God. This thief confessed his sin, and then justified Christ, saying, "This man hath done nothing amiss."

The next thing is, he had faith. Talk about faith, I think this is the most extraordinary case of faith in the Bible. We talk about Abraham as the father of the faithful; Abraham's faith cannot compare with this man's faith. God had Abraham twenty-five years talking up his faith. Moses saw the burning bush, and God talked with him; he had reason to believe. But this man we have no reason to believe ever knew anything about Christ. His disciples had heard his wonderful sermons and parables, and seen him perform his mighty works; and yet they had forsaken him. One of his chief men, Peter, had denied him with a curse; perhaps the thief heard this. Judas had betrayed him. He saw no glittering crown upon his brow; he could see where they had put the crown of thorns, and the scars they made; he could see no sign of his kingdom. If he had a kingdom, where were his subjects? They were wagging their heads; they were crying: "Save thyself, if Thou be King of the Jews." Yet that thief called him Lord. I consider that man had more faith than any other person mentioned in Scripture. When I was a boy I was a poor speller, but one day there came a word to the boy at the head of the class which he couldn't spell, and the word went down to the foot; none of the class could spell it. I spelled it, as we used to say then, by good luck; and I went from the foot of the class to the head. So the thief on the cross passed by Abraham, Moses and Elijah, and went to the head of the class. How refreshing it must have been to Christ to have one more own him as Lord, and believe he had a kingdom, and that he was a King. Oh, thank God for this man's testimony." He said unto Jesus, "Lord, remember me when thou comest into thy kingdom." If you are going to get into the kingdom of God, or if you are going to come to Christ, you must have faith in him.

The first thing this thief did, he feared God. Then he did not justify himself but justified Christ. "We, indeed, suffer justly, but this man hath done nothing amiss." Then his faith went out toward him; faith flashed into his soul. The moment he had faith in him he cried out: "Lord, remember me when thou comest into thy kingdom."

Because I said something here the other night about the Jews, I don't know how many abusive letters I have received. I have a thousand times more respect for the Jew, who will not believe in the Son of God, than I have for those who believe in him and will not trust him. This thief, the moment he did believe Christ was the Son of God, right there he owned him: "Lord, remember me." How many men in Philadelphia know he is the Son of God, but have not the moral courage to come out and call him Lord. This thief — ah, how noble! right there alone, no one standing by him — not even the thief on the other side. There was the chief priest, Caiaphas, and the chief men of his nation against him; and there was no one cared to speak out on that memorable hour, only that poor thief! I can imagine he had a praying mother, and that when he was a little boy his mother taught him the fifty-fifth chapter of Isaiah, and he learned that verse: "Seek ye the Lord while may be found; call ye upon him while he is near." When he found this was the Lord, he called upon him at once. A man said to me once: "I cannot make a prayer; I read prayers." What could this poor thief have done if he could not have made a prayer? He had no book; and if anyone had given him a book, he could not have read it. He prayed out of the heart. His prayer was short, but it brought the blessing; it came to the point: "Lord, remember me when thou comest into thy kingdom." He asked the Lord to give him, right there and then, what he wanted.

You see, in the conversion of this thief, that salvation is distinct and separate from works. Now some people tell us we have to work to be saved. What has the man who believes that to say about the salvation of this thief? How is he going to work, when he has nails through both hands and through both feet? He cannot work with his hands or run with his feet. When he had the use of his hands, they were lifted up to shed blood; and when he had the use of his feet, they were engaged in the service of the devil.

He took the Lord at his word, and believed. It is with the heart men believe, not with their hands or feet. All that is necessary for a man to be saved is, to believe with his heart. This thief made a good confession. If he had been a Christian fifty years, he could not have done Christ more service than he did there. He confessed him before the world; and for eighteen hundred years that confession had been told. Matthew, Mark, Luke and John have all recorded it. They felt it so important that they thought we should have it. Someone has said that Christ did not give the thief arms to fight for God, but he gave him wings that he might fly away to his Creator. He got an answer to his prayer as soon as he asked. He said, "Lord." He put the Lord at the head of the prayer. "Lord, remember me." Three short words — three golden links in that chain that bound him to the throne of God. The Lord could not help answering that prayer. He says he will save all that will call upon him; the man called upon him, and he had to answer the prayer. Did you ever see a man in the wide, wide world that ever called to the Lord out of the depths of his heart, that the Lord did not answer? The answer came.

See how salvation is separate and distinct from all ordinances — not but ordinances are right in their place. Some people say you cannot be saved if you are not baptized. Many people think it is impossible for any one to get into the kingdom of God if he is not baptized into it. I don't want you to think I am talking against ordinances. Baptism is right in its place; but when you put it in the place of salvation, you put a snare in the way. You cannot baptize men into the kingdom of God. The last conversion before Christ perished on the cross ought to forever settle that question. If you tell me a man cannot get into Paradise without being baptized, I answer, This thief was not baptized. If he had wanted to be baptized, I don't believe he could have found a man to baptize him. Some people tell us a man cannot be saved until he has partaken of the sacrament. The thief did not. Who administered the bread and wine to him? Was there a man on that mountain that would have faith to believe he could have been saved? Would the Roman government have allowed them to administer the sacrament, or baptism? The moment he asked for life he got it. Salvation is distinct from ordinances. Baptism is one thing; the Lord's Supper is another thing; and salvation through Christ is another. The only way for us to be saved is to come straight to Christ for life, and to own, as this man, that we have sinned, and that our condemnation is just.

Bear in mind, God is just; and the condemnation he has pronounced against us is a just condemnation. "The soul that sinneth it shall die." God has a right to put a penalty to his law, and it is just for God to pronounce condemnation. But God is also a God of mercy. God will have mercy upon all them that call upon him. I can imagine, after that thief believed, he commenced right there at once to praise God. I can imagine, as the soldier drove his spear into our Savior's side, there came flashing into his mind the words of the prophet Zechariah: "In that day there shall be a fountain opened to the house of David, and to the inhabitants of Jerusalem, for sin and for uncleanness." He was led out in the morning to the cross; in the evening he was in the Paradise of God, crowned with a crown he should wear through all ages. In the morning led out to suffer punishment; in the evening, going down the streets of Paradise, arm in arm with the Son of God. In the morning, not an eye to pity him; in the evening, up there amid the hallelujahs of heaven. In the morning, in the society of thieves; in the evening, washed and made clean in the blood of the Lamb.

You know Christ died a little while before the thief. I can imagine he wanted to hurry home to get a mansion for him, and to give him a welcome when he got there, that he should not be a stranger. The Lord loved him, because he confessed him in that dark hour. It was a dark hour for many of them who said, He is not the Son of God, the Savior of the world.

Some go so far as to try and make out he was an imposter. In this dark day, should we not come out like the thief and confess him, and take our stand on his side? If we do, he will remember it. The thief wanted to be remembered in Christ's kingdom. When Christ instituted the Lord's Supper, his dying request was we should remember him in this world; and now the thief's request was, that he might be remembered in his new kingdom. Go into some of our churches next Sunday morning, where they are going to administer the Lord's Supper. The bread and wine are there. The minister, who pronounces the benediction, asks the people to stay and partake of the Lord's Supper. Two-thirds of the people will get up and turn their backs upon it. They say: "What do I care for his death? What do I care for what the Son of God has done for me?" But this thief, thanks be to God! did confess him! He asked to be remembered; he believed Christ has a kingdom. Hundreds of thousands of people believe Christ has a kingdom; yet they will not seek him, and they will not cry out, "Lord, remember me." I believe that if every unsaved soul to-night in this hall would cry out, from the depths of his heart, "Lord, remember me," the answer would come this very night. Before I get through this sermon, the answer would come. He would remember you, and there would be the response, "This very night you shall become an heir of my kingdom." You can become this night a follower of the Lord Jesus Christ, if you will. I can imagine how the thief's soul leaped for joy when he heard Christ say, "It is finished." He wanted to follow him. I can imagine, when the men came to break the legs of these thieves, that this one was in a hurry to be gone. The moment his soul left that body, it leaped into a chariot sent down from heaven; and away it went to meet the Savior. He was a condemned man in the morning; in the evening in the Paradise of God. So if you have come in here without God and hope, as black in heart as that poor thief, if you call upon God, he will have mercy upon you and save you to-night. I have no doubt that, until he cried to the Lord, that thief had no thought that he would be saved. I have no doubt thousands come here without any thought of being saved; they come out of curiosity. I wish Christians would pray that the fear of the Lord would come to this audience, and that you may confess him, and take your place as a sinner, and ask God to remember you. He will remember you and make you an heir of his kingdom, if you accept of his salvation as a gift. This night, this hour, will you not call upon him — this hour, at the close of this meeting? Dear friends, what will you do with Jesus — with the Savior? He comes and he offers salvation. You can be saved now if you will. He is just the same Savior the thief had: it is the same cry he made that you want to make. Let that cry go up now. While I am speaking do you whisper, "Lord, Lord, remember me!" and see if he does not answer your prayer. Do you want the Lord to remember you, and have mercy upon you? Call upon him to-night. The thief was the first man to enter Paradise after the veil of the Temple was rent. If we could look up yonder, and see around the Throne; if we could catch a glimpse of the Throne, we should see the Father there and Jesus Christ at his right hand; but hard by the throne you should see that thief. He is there to-night. Eighteen hundred years he has been there, just because he cried: "Lord, remember me when thou comest into thy kingdom." I see Mary Magdalene there, and Zaccheus the chief publican of Jericho; and if I could ask them how they came there, they would shout down, "Saved by grace." There is only one way to heaven. O my friends, do you want to join that throng? Then send up the cry, "Lord, remember me." Oh, I pray to-night that hundreds may send up that cry.

PRAYER MEETING TALKS

BELIEF IN GOD – II KINGS 7

I have believed in God for thirty years. When first converted I did not believe in him very much, but ever since then I have believed in him, more and more every year. When people come to me, tell me they can't believe, and ask what they shall do, I tell them to do as I once knew a man to do. He went and knelt down and told God honestly he could not believe in him, and I advise them to go off alone and tell it right out to the Lord. But if you stop to ask yourself why you don't believe in him, is there really any reason? People read infidel books and wonder why they are unbelievers, I ask why they read such books. They think they must read both sides. I say that book is a lie; how can it be one side when it is a lie? It is not one side at all. Suppose a man tells down right lies about my family, and I read them so as to hear both sides; it would not be long before some suspicion would creep into my mind. I said to a man once, "Have you got a wife?" "Yes, and a good one." I asked: "Now what if I should come to you and cast out insinuations against her?" And he said, "Well your life would not be safe long if you did." I told him just to treat the devil as he would treat a man who went round with such stories. We are not to blame for having doubts flitting through our minds, but for harboring them. Let us go out trusting the Lord with heart and soul to-day.

TRUE FRIENDSHIP

We read in the 15th chapter of 11th Samuel that David was

fleeing in exile from Jerusalem. Absalom had already undermined his power and superseded him on the throne. But as David went through the gate six hundred men passed on before him, and the king said to Ittai, the leader: "Wherefore goest thou also with us; return to thy place and abide with the king, for thou art a stranger and also an exile." And Ittai answered the king and said, "As the Lord liveth, and as my lord the king liveth, surely in what place my lord the king shall be, whether in death or life, even there also will thy servant be." There was another man, too, called Hushai, who went out to meet the king, but he returned again to the city. How it must have pleased David to have found Ittai outside the gate. Ittai is worth thousands of Hushais. David did not know who his friends were until trouble came. There was true fellowship, true love in that act. In time of distress Ittai would not desert his king, but followed him into exile. So it should be in the church. That is just what Christ looks for; the only thing which can please him is the true love that will leave all to follow him. Some people do not know the meaning of the word fellowship — it means partnership. Our partnership is with Christ the Son, and when we come into it everything we have belongs to the firm; we can do nothing by ourselves without consulting Christ. We must be like Ittai, willing to leave the city and all we possess, if necessary, to follow him.

JOSEPH OF ARIMATHEA

What I want to call attention to this morning is how one act done for Christ, with a pure motive, will live forever. All four of the disciples give an account of this deed. Joseph of Arimathea, was a rich man and a counselor, a good and just man, and John tells us he had long been a secret disciple of Christ. He had never come out boldly for fear of the Jews, but in that hour, when all had deserted him and one had betrayed him, the death of Christ brought Joseph out, and he alone came forward to care for the crucified body. It is the death of Christ which should enlist us all. The fact that he died for us should make us all come forward to advance his kingdom. Joseph had been opposed to the death of Jesus, but he had taken no part in his trial and crucifixion. Dr. Bonner says, "When you have a trial before a committee and one of its members will oppose the measure you want to carry, you don't send for him — you have the meeting without him if you can." So when this matter came up before the Sanhedrim, Joseph was not there and was not sent for. It is only when Christ is dead upon the cross that Joseph comes forward as a disciple and begs the body of Pilate — an act which has lived nearly one thousand nine hundred years, and which will continue to live throughout all time. Matthew, Mark, and Luke do not tell us where Joseph got the myrrh and aloes, but John tells us Nicodemus brought a hundred pounds weight, and that they put linen clothes upon the body of Jesus, with the spices, and laid it in a new sepulchre wherein was never man yet laid. It was a tomb Joseph had built for himself, expecting to lie there some day, but he probably thought the sepulchre would be all the sweeter if Christ had laid there.

When we go away from here, let us see what we can do for the sake of Jesus, what acts that deserve to live.

OUR REFUGE

I want to call your attention to the six cities of refuge appointed by Joshua for the children of Israel. These cities were set apart that all men who killed any person unawares or unwittingly, and without hatred, might flee to them and be safe within their gates. The magistrates had to see to it that guide-boards were put up, stones cleared away, and the roads kept clear for those who fled for their lives from the avengers of blood. These ancient cities of refuge are in our day represented by Christ. He is our refuge in all times of trouble.

The names of the cities are Hebrew, and all have a meaning.

Kedish means holiness. If we flee to this city of refuge we will be made holy. Had Christ committed sin we could have no hope, but since he is without sin, if we are in Christ we are made perfect. Shechem meant shoulder, which means strength and power. If a man needs strength he must flee there. Sins are in one of two places, on us or on Christ. If we are weak we must find strength in Shechem. Hebron means joined. If we can get there we are joint heirs with Jesus Christ. Beser means fortified; you are secured there if you want to get away from the world. Ramoth means heights and Golan means exile — exile in this world and citizenship in heaven. These six cities ought to be a help to you. Have we Christ for our refuge? If a man is away from God, what hope has he? It is folly for a man who has an appetite for drink to try and overcome it by himself; he can't overcome both his appetite and the devil alone. It is only through Christ that we can be secure.

THE HOLY SPIRIT

If we have the Spirit, we have the fruit of the Spirit. If the Spirit of God is in us, we will have these qualities of his Spirit. "He that loveth not, knoweth not God; for God is love." Some one said to me the other day that he understood about belief, but could not understand what it was to be born again. I told him that he that believed had life eternal, and whoever received life through Christ was born again. A man cannot get that life by merely going to church and observing forms; he must get the Spirit of God, and then he will have light and peace. We have no peace so long as we have sin, but if we accept Christ, and salvation through him, our sins are blotted out, and we have peace in reviewing the past. Spiritual power is what we want next. As soon as the Holy Ghost comes we want boldness to go out and proclaim Jesus. There was once a man on trial for his life. The king of the country in which he lived said the law must take its course, but, after he was tried and condemned, he would pardon him. The man was cool all through his trial, and when they brought in a verdict of guilty, the man was perfectly unconcerned. So with the Christian. He will have boldness in his heart on the day of judgment, because he knows Christ became a propitiation for his sins and he has his pardon laid up in his heart.

THREE CLASSES

I always notice many here at noon whom we have met in the inquiry-rooms, and I want to speak a word to them. There are three classes of people who will not accept salvation — those who neglect it, those who refuse it, and those who despise it. Many think they are not so bad as the scoffer at religion because they only neglect it, but if they keep on they are lost just the same. Suppose there is a man in a boat going in a swift current down the stream; if he neglects to pull for the shore he is a doomed man. He will go over the rapids, won't he? If Noah had neglected to go into the ark after he had built it, he would have been lost with the other antediluvians. Nothing could have saved him. You let the cry be raised that this buiding is on fire, and see how many will keep their seats; they would be burned up as sure as they did.

Then again in the 12th chapter of Hebrews, 25th verse, "See that ye refuse not him that speaketh." The next step is to refuse salvation. A while ago they only neglected it, now they refuse it — that is the second round of the ladder. You can only do one of two things, take it or refuse it. You have all been in a house where the waiter passed ice-water to a number of people sitting together, and seen how some would take it and some would not; so the cup of salvation is passed among you to-day. How many of you will accept it? Are you almost persuaded? Remember a hair's breadth from heaven is not an inch from hell.

Again, in the 10th chapter of Hebrews, 28th verse, we read: "He that despised Moses's law died without mercy under two or three witnesses." Many despise the whole thing, hate it, and will have none of it — give them a tract and they light their cigars with it. There are the three words — neglect, refuse, despise. When there is but one engine and three cars attached, don't they all go the same way? If you do either of these three things, you must suffer the eternal consequences.

BIBLE READINGS

THE GOSPEL INVITATION

I WILL read from Matthew 11:27:

"All things are delivered unto me of my Father; and no man knoweth the Son but the Father; neither knoweth any man the Father, save the Son, and he to whomsoever the Son will reveal him. Come unto me, all ye that labor and are heavy laden, and I will give you rest. Take my yoke upon you, and learn of me; for I am meek and lowly in heart; and ye shall find rest unto your souls. For my yoke is easy, and my burden is light." Luke 15th: "Then drew near unto him all the publicans and sinners for to hear him; and the Pharisees and scribes murmured, saying, This man receiveth sinners, and eateth with them." The Pharisees would tell the truth now and then; and they never told a more truthful thing than that. That is the glory of the gospel of Jesus Christ. He came into the world for sinners. He came to seek and to save that which was lost; so, when the Pharisees said this, they told the truth once, if they never did before. There is one more text that I want to refer to, in the 6th chapter of John, 37: "Him that cometh unto me, I will in no wise cast out."

Now when princes and kings of this earth generally call people round them, they generally call the great and mighty and the noble; but when the Prince of Peace was here, he called publicans and sinners; many of them were outcasts, whom most of the people would not associate with. He was all the time calling around him all classes. There is one passage of Scripture which is very precious to me, and that is, that Christ helped all men that had need of him. Now if there is a man here to-day who has need of Christ, he will help him. Any man or woman in this assembly that needs Christ, can have him. He will give you all the help you need; I don't care what your besetting sin is. It may be your appetite for strong drink. Bring that to him; he has got power to take that from you. Now, a good many think they would like to come to Christ, but they want to get ready first; they want to lop off this sin and that sin, and stop swearing and drinking, and then they will be ready. That would be like a sick man waiting until he was well, and then sending for a physician; or like a blind man waiting until he recovers his sight, and then sending for a doctor. You bring your sickness and your blindness to Christ, and then he will help you. It is the sick that need a physician, and not those who are well. And if there is a man here troubled with any besetting sin, I don't care what it is, let him come to Christ, and he will help him; for he has promised, "Him that cometh unto me, I will in no wise cast out." I like those *I wills*; they are all good. You cannot find a man that can honestly and truthfully say that he came to Christ and he didn't receive him, and he cast him out. No man living can say that; because he has received all that have come, and all that will come.

There was a man in our late war, and as he lay upon his cot (he was a skeptical man), there was one of those silent messengers hanging on the wall of the hospital; and this was the text, "Him that cometh unto me, I will in no wise cast out." One day he got a letter from his mother, and was so sick he could not read it, but the nurse read it to him; and this letter was an earnest appeal to her boy to accept of Christ. He was down there in the hospital, and she didn't know but he would die without her seeing him again; and she quoted that text to him: "Him that cometh unto me, I will in no wise cast out."

The dying man said: "That is very singular; there it is on the wall, and my mother has written it." A day or two after he was much worse, and sinking rapidly; and he asked the nurse to read his mother's letter again. And when she got to that text, he said, "Did mother put that in the letter, 'Him that cometh unto me, I will in no wise cast out?'" "Yes," says the nurse. "And does the Bible say it?" "Yes." "And if mother says it and the Bible says it, it must be true." And, dear friends, he believed and received Christ.

It is true. Take it just as you are: "Him that cometh unto me, I will in no wise cast out." May God help every man in this assembly, and every woman to come with all their sins; and the Lord will take you to his loving bosom, and will hold you, and keep you until that day.

DIVINITY OF JESUS

We come to-day to the 8th chapter of the gospel according to John. In this chapter Christ asserts his divinity; and I do not see how any one can read the 8th chapter of John and not believe in the Divinity of the Lord Jesus Christ. The next morning after he had been, as it were, driven out of Jerusalem, he came back into the Temple. It says in the last verse of the 7th chapter: "And every man went unto his own house. But Jesus went into the Mount of Olives." But early the next morning, he came into the Temple; and they brought a woman in to see what he would say should be done with her. He had been teaching that he had come not to condemn, but to save. The law of Moses condemned this poor fallen woman to death; and now they tried to entangle him, and see what he would do with her. When he had put the test to these men, and they had all gone out, he said to her, "Neither will I condemn thee; go, and sin no more." Moses or Elijah, or any of the prophets, could not have said that; no man living could have said that: "Neither do I condemn thee; go, and sin no more." In the 12th verse he says, "I am the light of the world." Moses could not say, I am the light of the world.

Abraham could not say it; no other man could say that. I said to my little boy, seven years old, this morning, as I was reading this chapter, "Willie, who could say that?" He answered; "Jesus." "Who else?" "God." "Who else?" "No one else." "I am the light of the world; if any man follow me, he will not walk in darkness, but will have the light of life." Who can give the light but God? In the morning of creation, he said, "Let there be light;" and there was light. Now Christ comes, and proclaims himself the light of the world. It would be a great help to us in reading the Bible, just to get this into our minds, that Christ was God and man. Sometimes he spoke as man, and sometimes as God. That gives us a key to the Holy Bible; but take it away, and I do not see how you are going to understand it. Without it, it is a sealed book. Some people accuse us of teaching that God died; but Christ died as a man. God never died, and never can die; it was the man that died. Men die; the Divinity never dies. Then he says again, "I am not alone;" "I go my way;" "I am from above." Who could say that but him? "I am from above; I am not of this world." Who else could say that, if he hadn't come down from the world above? "If ye believe not that I am he, ye shall die in your sins." "I speak to the world those things which I have heard of him." When did he hear them, if he hadn't come from the bosom of the Father? "When ye have lifted up the Son of man, then shall ye know that I am he, and that I do nothing of myself: but as my father has taught me, I speak these things."

Then in the 30th verse: "As he spake these words many believed on him." How simple that was! As he stood there, speaking to them in the Temple, many were converted and believed on him. God received them right there, while he was speaking. How simple the conversions of the Bible are! Simply believing, simply receiving. Then in the 36th verse: "If the Son, therefore, shall make you free, ye shall be free indeed." If he were not God, how was he going to make us free from sin? But, "If the Son, therefore, shall make you free, ye shall be free indeed." I think there are a good many of God's children who never have got to that verse. They don't know what freedom is. They are still asleep, and sunk in bondage. They are like Lazarus, who got out of the grave with his grave clothes on, bound hand and foot. The difficulty with those people is, that they are always looking in their own hearts to get freedom; but it is the truth which makes us free — the Word of God. Miss Smiley was telling about going down South, a few years after the war. She went to a hotel, and the room she was shown to was not very clean. She said to the colored woman who was there: "I would like to have you fix it up; I am from the North, and you know the Northern people set you free." She went away and came back in a little while; and it seemed as if half a day's work had been done. "Now," said the colored woman, "bees I free or beent I? My old master tells me I am not free; and I go out among the colored people, and they say I am free." There are a great many of God's people just that way; they do not know whether they are free or not. It is not a matter of feeling. The proclamation of Abraham Lincoln set that woman free; and so it is the proclamation of God's Word that makes us free; not that we feel this way or that way. If we want liberty in Christ, we can have it. When he told them that, they said: "We are the descendants of Moses and Abraham; we have not been in bondage to anybody." And all that time they were under the Roman yoke. So, hundreds of men in Boston to-day, who are bound hand and foot to something in this world, do not want to become Christians, because they think they will not have their liberty. The truth will make you free. That is the only freedom worth having: "and if the truth makes you free, you are free indeed." Then again he said, "I speak that which I have seen with my Father." He talked about the mansions above, as freely as Queen Victoria's children would talk about the rooms in Windsor castle. He was familiar with those scenes. "But now ye seek to kill me, a man that hath told you the truth, which I have heard of God." Then again he told them: "I proceeded forth from God"; that was his own testimony. Then again, "I tell you the truth." I tell it to you, it is the truth. "I honor my Father"; "I have come to honor him"; "I have come to do thy will, O God"; "I seek not my own glory; I seek to glorify my Father"; "I say unto you, if any man keep my saying, he shall never see death." Of course, he is not speaking about the death of the body, but about the death of the soul. "If any man keep my saying, he shall never see death." His words are the words of life: and if a man receives them, he will not die.

Let us read these few verses closing this chapter.

"Verily, verily, I say unto you, If a man keep my sayings he shall never see death. Then said the Jews unto him, Now we know that thou hast a devil. Abraham is dead, and the prophets; and thou sayest, If a man keep my sayings, he shall never taste of death. Art thou greater than our Father Abraham, which is dead? And the prophets are dead; whom makest thou thyself? Jesus answered, If I honor myself, my honor is nothing; it is my Father that honoreth me, of whom ye say that he is your God. Yet ye have not known him; but I know him; and if I should say, I know him not, I shall be a liar unto you; but I know him and keep his saying. Your father Abraham rejoiced to see my day, and he saw it, and was glad. Then said the Jews unto him, Thou art not yet fifty years old, and hast thou seen Abraham? Jesus said unto them, Verily, verily, I say unto you, Before Abraham was, I am."

This forever settles in my mind the question of the divinity of the Lord Jesus. "Before Abraham was, I am." How any man can read the gospel of John and be in any doubt about Christ's divinity, I cannot see. Abraham was gone hundreds of years;

and yet, "Before Abraham was, I am." "Then they took up stones to cast at him; but Jesus hid himself, and went out of the Temple, going through the midst of them, and so passed by."

PRAYERS OF JESUS

I will just read a few verses of Scripture, and then the meeting will be thrown open. We want to hear from as many as possible, and we want a good deal of prayer. We felt that the meetings of the Tabernacle were too large; and we would rather have small meetings, where friends could pray. I do not believe there is any true revival that is not brought about by a good deal of prayer; and if we have a work of grace that is going to be deep and thorough in this city, we have got to have more prayer than we have had. I want to call your attention, to-day, to the prayers of Jesus Christ. Although he was God, yet he was man; as man he prayed, and as God he answered prayer. And he encouraged others to come to him with their burdens; and he was constantly praying, because he was an example to others. In the 3d chapter of Luke, 21st verse, we find that when he was baptized he was praying. Now, when all the people were baptized, it came to pass that Jesus also being baptized, and praying, the heaven was opened. And the Holy Ghost descended in a bodily shape like a dove upon him; and a voice came from heaven, which said, Thou art my beloved Son, in whom I am well pleased."

Then we read again in Luke, 9:28, how he took Peter, James and John and went up into the Mountain of Transfiguration; and while he was praying, his countenance was transfigured, and there came a voice saying: "This is my beloved Son, in whom I am well pleased." In John, 12:27, we find him praying again; it was when they were about to kill him: "Now is my soul troubled; and what shall I say? Father, save me from this hour; but for this cause came I unto this hour. Father, glorify thy name. Then came there a voice from heaven, saying, I have both glorified it, and will glorify it again." In Luke 22:42, 43, we find him praying, and He sweat, as it were, great drops of blood, and as he prayed an angel appeared to Him and strengthened Him. And we find that these four times which are recorded, when He was praying he heard from heaven; it was really his prayers that opened heaven. As it was with Stephen, when he was dying he prayed, and the heavens opened before him. Now if we are going to have the windows of heaven opened, and the Spirit of God descending in mighty power upon this city, it is going to be in answer to prayer and earnest supplications. Then, in the 6th chapter of Luke and the 12th verse, before he chose his disciples, it was a matter of prayer to him: "And it came to pass in those days that He went out into a mountain to pray, and continued all night in prayer to God" — continued all night. "And when it was day, He called unto him his disciples; and of them He chose twelve, whom also he named apostles." So the night before he chose those twelve that were to shake the world, and be a blessing to the world and establish the Church of God on earth, He spent that night in prayer. And so, my friends, if we are going to do a great work for God, we must spend much time in prayer; we have got to be closeted with God. We find him again at the grave of Lazarus; and He prayed before He called him forth. It was in answer to prayer that Lazarus was raised.

And then, if you will turn into the 17th chapter of John, in that wonderful prayer of Christ, you will find seven requests there. We talk about the disciple's prayer as the Lord's prayer; really the Lord's prayer is this 17th chapter of John. That was his last prayer that has been recorded, except the one on the cross; and in this 17th chapter of John, there are seven requests. There is only one for himself; four for the disciples that were around him; and two for you and I, and for all that should believe on him afterwards. And then we find him saying to Peter, "I have prayed for thee that thy strength fail thee not."

When Satan was to sift him, Christ had prayed for him; and how that must have cheered and encouraged Peter after his fall, to think that Christ had told him he was going to pray for him; and his prayers did prevail, and Peter was brought back. And then the last breath on the cross, just before he cried, "It is finished," and gave up the ghost! It was a prayer, "Father, forgive them, for they know not what they do." He was a man of prayer; and let the business men of Boston imitate their Master. We that are Christians, let us imitate God, and let us lay hold on God in prayer to-day, that He may give us a great and mighty blessing. Let us all pray.

LIFE, LOVE, PEACE, POWER, BOLDNESS

I will read a few verses from the 1st Epistle of John, 4th chapter, beginning at the 7th verse:

"Beloved, let us love one another, for love is of God; and every one that loveth is born of God, and knoweth God. He that loveth not, knoweth not God, for God is love. In this was manifested the love of God toward us, because that God sent his only begotten Son into the world that we might live through him. Herein is love, not that we loved God, but that he loved us, and sent his Son to be the propitiation for our sins. Beloved, if God so loved us, we ought also to love one another. No man hath seen God at any time. If we love one another, God dwelleth in us, and his love is perfected in us. Hereby know we that we dwell in him and he in us, because he hath given us of his Spirit. And we have seen and do testify that the Father sent the Son to be the Savior of the world. Whosoever shall confess that Jesus is the Son of God, God dwelleth in him, and he in God. And we have known and believe the love that God hath to us. God is love; and he that dwelleth in love, dwelleth in God, and God in him. Herein is our love made perfect, that we may have boldness in the day of judgment; because as he is, so are we in this world.

There is no fear in love, but perfect love casteth out fear; because fear hath torment. He that feareth is not made perfect in love. We love him because he first loved us. If a man say, I love God, and hateth his brother, he is a liar. For he that loveth not his brother, whom he hath seen, how can he love God, whom he hath not seen? And this commandment have we from him, That he who loveth God, love his brother also."

In these few words I have read to you, there are a few thoughts I want to call to your attention to; I might say five things, that are necessary for every Christian to have. The first is *life*. We get that in the 9th verse: "God sent his only begotten Son into the world, that we might live through him." Now, there is no life, no spiritual life, till we know Christ; or, in other words, Christ is that life himself. There are a good many people now that are troubled about the new birth; they want to know what it means. To be born again is to have Christ in the soul, that is the new birth; and with that life we serve God. And we cannot serve God till Christ is formed in us — the hope of glory. That is the life that all want. Our prayers are not prayers till Christ is there; with that life we serve him. Then the next thing we get is in the 10th verse, that sin is put away. That is *peace*. What every Christian wants is, peace to the soul. He gets that by knowing that sin has been atoned for, propitiation made. Christ has forever settled the question of sin; it has been put away; we are at rest as we look back to Calvary, knowing the cross has put away sin. We are ready to serve God, because sin is out of the way. The next thing is in the 11th verse: "Beloved, if God so loved us, we ought also to love one another." We have got to have *love*. You cannot do a man any good unless you love him. Let us see if we have life, peace, and love. The next thing is *power*. We get that in the 13th verse: "Hereby know we that we dwell in him, and he in us, because he hath given us of his Spirit." That is power. There is really no power without the Holy Ghost; it is Holy Ghost power that we want.

We want the Holy Ghost resting on us for service. Many of you have passed through experiences of how easy it is to talk for God when the Holy Ghost is resting in you for service; and how hard it has been when you had no power. Perhaps sin has come between you and God, and, of course, then the power is gone. Therefore let us see that we have that qualification. Then the next thing is *boldness*. That is one of the traits that a great many lack, at the present time. There is so much scoffing and ridicule that many, if you will allow me the use of the expression, haven't backbone enough to stand up and confess Christ boldly, wherever their lot may be cast. We find that, in the 17th verse: "Herein is our love made perfect that we may have boldness in the day of judgment." We want it now while Christ is being misrepresented and laughed about; and if we have it here, we will have in the day of judgment; for Christ is with us. We are on the Lord's side, and we are always in the majority when we are with God. The idea that there are only a few that serve God is a false one. Let us be full of boldness and courage. If a man is once forgiven he can look up and say, Heaven is my home; God is my Father; Christ is my Savior; and he has nothing to fear. Let us speak out boldly for Christ.

THE CALL OF MOSES

THERE IS A great deal more room given in Scripture to the *call* of men to God's work than there is to their *end*. For instance, we don't know where Isaiah died, or how he died, but we know a great deal about the call God gave him, when he saw God on high and lifted up on His throne. I suppose that it is true to-day that hundreds of young men and women who are listening for a call and really want to know what their life's mission is, perhaps find it the greatest problem they ever had. Some don't know just what profession or work to take up, and so I should like to take the call of Moses, and see if we cannot draw some lessons from it.

You remember when God met Moses at the burning bush and called him to do as great a work as any man has ever been called to in this world, that

HE THOUGHT THE LORD HAD MADE A MISTAKE,

that he was not the man. He said, "Who am I?" He was very small in his own estimation. Forty years before he had started out as a good many others have started. He thought he was pretty well equipped for service. He had been in the schools of the Egyptians, he had been in the palaces of Egypt, he had moved in the *bon ton* society. He had had all the advantages any man could have when he started out, undoubtedly, without calling on the God of Abraham for wisdom and guidance, yet he broke down.

How many men have started out in some profession and

made a failure of it! They haven't heard the voice of God, they haven't waited upon God for instruction.

I suppose Moses thought that the children of Israel would be greatly honored to know that a prince of the realm was going to take up their cause, but you remember how he lost his temper and killed the Egyptian, and next day, when he interfered in a quarrel between two Hebrews, they wanted to know who had made him judge and ruler over them, and he had to flee into the desert, and was there for forty years hidden away. He killed the Egyptian and lost his influence thereby. Murder for liberty; wrong for right; it was a poor way to reform abuses, and Moses needed training.

It was a long time for God to keep him in His school, a long time for a man to wait in the prime of his life, from forty to eighty. Moses had been brought up with all the luxuries that Egypt could give him, and now he was a shepherd, and in the sight of the Egyptians a shepherd was an abomination. I have an idea that Moses started out with a great deal bigger head than heart. I believe that is the reason so many fail; they have

BIG HEADS AND LITTLE HEARTS.

If a man has a shriveled-up heart and a big head he is a monster. Perhaps Moses looked down on the Hebrews. There are many people who start out with the idea that they are great and other people are small, and they are going to bring them up on the high level with themselves. God never yet used a man of that stamp. Perhaps Moses was a slow scholar in God's school, and so He had to keep him there for forty years.

But now he is ready; he is just the man God wants, and God calls him. Moses said, "Who am I?" He was very small in his own eyes — just small enough so that God could use him. If you had asked the Egyptians who he was, they would have said he was

THE BIGGEST FOOL IN THE WORLD.

"Why," they would say, "look at the opportunity that man had! He might have been commander of the Egyptian army, he might have been on the throne, swaying the sceptre over the whole world, if he hadn't identified himself with those poor, miserable Hebrews! Think what an opportunity he has lost, and what a privilege he has thrown away!"

He had dropped out of the public mind for forty years, and they didn't know what had become of him, but God had His eye upon him. He was the very man of all others that God wanted, and when he met God with that question, "Who am I?" it didn't matter who *he* was but who his God was. When men learn the lesson that they are nothing and God is everything, then there is not a position in which God cannot use them. It was not Moses who accomplished that great work of redemption, for he was only the instrument in God's hand. God could have spoken to Pharaoh without Moses. He could have spoken in a voice of thunder, and broken the heart of Pharaoh with one speech, if He had wanted to, but He condescended to take up a human agent, and to use him. He could have sent Gabriel down, but he knew that Moses was the man wanted above all others, so He called him. God uses men to speak to men; He works through mediators. He could have accomplished the exodus of the children of Israel in a flash, but instead He chose to send a lonely and despised shepherd to work out His purpose through pain and disappointment. That was God's way in the Old Testament, and also in the New. He sent His own Son in the likeness of sinful flesh to be the mediator between God and man.

Moses went on making excuses and said, "When I go down there, who shall I say has sent me?" I suppose he remembered how he went before he was sent that other time, and he was afraid of a failure again. A man who has made a failure once is always afraid he will make another. He loses confidence in himself. It is a good thing to lose confidence in ourselves so as to gain confidence in God.

The Lord said, "Say unto them, 'I AM hath sent me.'"

Some one has said that God gave him

A BLANK CHECK,

and all he had to do was fill it out from that time on. When he wanted to bring water out of the rock, all he had to do was to fill out the check; when he wanted bread, all he had to do was to fill out the check and the bread came; he had a rich banker. God had taken him into partnership with Himself. God had made him His heir, and all he had to do was to look up to Him, and he got all he wanted.

And yet he seemed to draw back, and began to make another excuse, and said:

"They will not believe me."

He was afraid of the Israelites as well as of Pharaoh: he knew how hard it is to get even your friends to believe in you.

Now, if God has sent you and me with a message it is not for us to say whether others will believe it or not. *We* cannot make men believe. If I have been sent by God to make men believe, He will give me power to make them believe. Jesus Christ didn't have that power; it is the work of the Holy Ghost; we cannot persuade men and overcome skepticism and infidelity unless we are baptised with the Holy Ghost and with power.

God told Moses that they *would* believe him, that he would succeed, and bring the children of Israel out of bondage. But Moses seemed to distrust even the God who had spoken to him.

Then the Lord said, "What is that in thy hand?"

He had a rod or staff, a sort of shepherd's crook, which he had cut haphazard when he had wanted something that would serve him in the desert.

"It is only a rod."

"With that you shall deliver the children of Israel; with that rod you shall make Israel believe that I am with you."

When God Almighty linked Himself to that rod, it was worth more than all the armies the world had ever seen. Look and see how that rod did its work. It brought up the plagues of flies, and the thunder storm, and turned the water into blood. It was not Moses, however, nor Moses' rod that did the work, but it was the God of the rod, the God of Moses. As long as God was with him, he could not fail.

Sometimes it looks as if God's servants fail. When Herod beheaded John the Baptist, it looked as if John's mission was a failure. But was it? The voice that rang through the valley of the Jordan rings through the whole world to-day. You can hear its echo upon the mountains and the valleys yet, "I must decrease, but He must increase." He held up Jesus Christ and introduced Him to the world, and Herod had not power to behead him until his life work had been accomplished. Stephen never preached but one sermon that we know of, and that was before the Sanhedrim; but how that sermon has been preached again and again all over the world! Out of his death probably came Paul, the greatest preacher the world has seen since Christ left this earth. If a man is sent by Jehovah, there is no such thing as failure. Was Christ's life a failure? See how His parables are going through the earth to-day. It looked as if the apostles had made a failure, but see how much has been accomplished. If you read the book of Acts, you will see that every seeming failure in Acts was turned into a great victory. Moses wasn't going to fail, although Pharaoh said with contempt, "Who is God that I should obey Him?" He found out who God was. He found out that there was a God.

But Moses made another excuse, and said, "I am slow of speech, slow of tongue." He said he was

NOT AN ORATOR.

My friends, we have too many orators. I am tired and sick of your "silver-tongued orators." I used to mourn because I couldn't be an orator. I thought, Oh, if I could only have the gift of speech like some men! I have heard men with a smooth flow of language take the audience captive, but they came and they went, their voice was like the air, there wasn't any *power* back of it; they trusted in their eloquence and their fine speeches. That is what Paul was thinking of when he wrote to the Corinthians: — "My speech and my preaching was not with enticing words of man's wisdom, but in demonstration of the Spirit and of power: that your faith should not stand in the wisdom of men, but in the power of God."

Take a witness in court and let him try his oratorical powers in the witness-box, and see how quickly the judge will rule him out. It is the man who tells the plain, simple truth that has the most influence with the jury.

Suppose that Moses had prepared a speech for Pharaoh, and had got his hair all smoothly brushed, and had stood before the looking-glass or had gone to an elocutionist to be taught how to make an oratorical speech and how to make gestures. Suppose that he had buttoned his coat, put one hand in his chest, had struck an attitude and begun:

"The God of our fathers, the God of Abraham, Isaac, and Jacob, has commanded me to come into the presence of the noble King of Egypt."

I think they would have taken his head right off! They had Egyptians who could be as eloquent as Moses. It was not eloquence they wanted. When you see a man in the pulpit trying to show off his eloquence he is making a fool of himself and trying to make a fool of the people. Moses was slow of speech, but he had a message, and what God wanted was to have him deliver the message. But he insisted upon having an excuse. He didn't want to go; instead of being eager to act as heaven's messenger, to be God's errand boy, he wanted to excuse himself. The Lord humored him and gave him an interpreter, gave him Aaron.

Now, if there is a stupid thing in the world, it is to talk through an interpreter. I tried it once in Paris. I got up into a little box of a pulpit with the interpreter — there was hardly room enough for one. I said a sentence while he leaned away over to one side, and then I leaned over while he repeated it in French. Can you conceive of a more stupid thing than Moses going before Pharaoh and speaking through Aaron!

But this slow-of-speech man became eloquent. Talk about Gladstone's power to speak! Here is a man one hundred and twenty years old, and he waxed eloquent, as we see in Deuteronomy 32:1-4:

> Give ear, O ye heavens, and I will speak;
> And hear, O earth, the words of my mouth.
> My doctrine shall drop as the rain,
> My speech shall distil as the dew,
> As the small rain upon the tender herb,
> And as the showers upon the grass:
> Because I will publish the name of the Lord:
> Ascribe ye greatness unto our God.
> He is the Rock, His work is perfect:
> For all His ways are judgment:
> A God of truth and without iniquity,
> Just and right is He.

He turned out to be one of the most eloquent men the world has ever seen. If God sends men and they deliver His message He will be with their mouth. If God has given you a message, go and give it to the people as God has given it to you. It is a stupid thing for a man to try to be eloquent. Make

YOUR MESSAGE, AND NOT YOURSELF,

the most prominent thing. Don't be self-conscious. Set your heart on what God has given you to do, and don't be so foolish as to let your own difficulties or your own abilities stand in the way. It is said that people would go to hear Cicero and would come away and say, "Did you ever hear anything like it? wasn't it sublime? wasn't it grand?" But they would go and hear Demosthenes, and he would fire them so with the subject that they would want to go and fight at once. They forgot all about Demosthenes, but were stirred by his message, that was the difference between the two men.

Next Moses said: "O my Lord, send, I pray thee, by the hand of him whom thou wilt send."

Did you ever stop to think what Moses would have lost if God had taken him at his word, and said:

"Very well, Moses; you may stay here in the desert, and I will send Aaron, or Joshua, or Caleb!"

Don't seek to be excused if God calls you to some service. What would the twelve disciples have lost if they had declined the call of Jesus! I have always pitied those other disciples of whom we read that they went back, and walked no more with Jesus. Think what Orpah missed and what Ruth gained by cleaving to Naomi's God! Her story has been

TOLD THESE THREE THOUSAND YEARS.

Father, mother, sisters, brothers, the grave of her husband — she turned her back on them all. Ruth, come back, and tell us if you regret your choice! No: her name shines one of the brightest among all the women that have ever lived. The Messiah was one of her descendants.

Moses, you come back and tell us if you were afterwards sorry that God had called you? I think that when he stood in glorified body on the Mount of Transfiguration with Jesus and Elijah, he did not regret it.

My dear friends, God is not confined to any one messenger. We are told that He can raise up children out of stones. Some one has said that there are three classes of people, the "wills," the "won'ts," and the "can'ts"; the first accomplish everything, the second oppose everything, and the third fail in everything. If God calls you, consider it a great honor. Consider it a great privilege to have partnership with Him in anything. Do it cheerfully, gladly. Do it with all your heart, and He will bless you. Don't let false modesty or insincerity, self-interest, or any personal consideration turn you aside from the path of duty and sacrifice. If we listen for God's voice, we shall hear the call; and if He calls and sends us, there will be no such thing as failure, but success all along the line. Moses had glorious success because he went forward and did what God called him to do.

DEVOTIONS

As my Father hath sent me, even so send I you. — John 20:21

W E SHOULD never leave our room until we have seen the face of our dear Master, Christ, and have realized that we are being sent forth by Him to do His will, and to finish the work which He has given us to do. He who said to His immediate followers, "As my Father hath sent me, even so send I you," says as much to each one of us, as the dawn summons us to live another day. We should realize that we are as much sent forth by Him as the angels who "do His commandments, hearkening unto the voice of His word." There is some plan for each day's work, which He will unfold to us, if only we will look up to Him to do so; some mission to fulfil; some ministry to perform; some lesson patiently to learn, that we may be able to "reach others also." As to our plans we need not be anxious; because He who sends us forth is responsible to make the plan, according to His infinite wisdom; and to reveal it to us, however dull and stupid our faculties may be. And as to our sufficiency, we are secure of having all needful grace; because He never sends us forth, except He first breathes on us and says, "Receive ye the Holy Ghost." There is always a special endowment for special power. — *F. L. Meyer.*

A fountain . . . for sin and uncleanness. — Zech. 13:1

You that have faith in the Fountain, *frequent it.* Beware of two errors which are very natural and very disastrous. Beware of thinking any sin too great for it; beware of thinking any sin too small. There is not a sin so little, but it may be the germ of everlasting perdition; there is not a sin so enormous, but a drop of atoning blood will wash it away as utterly as if it were drowned in the depths of the sea. — *James Hamilton*

I am black ... as the tents of Kedar. — Song of Sol. 1:5
I am my beloved's, and his desire is toward me.

— Song of Sol. 7:10

Nothing humbles the soul like sacred and intimate communion with the Lord; yet there is a sweet joy in feeling that *He* knows *all,* and, nothwithstanding, loves us still. —*J. Hudson Taylor*

David enquired of the Lord. — II Sam. 5:19

Christian, if thou wouldst know the path of duty, take God for thy compass; if thou wouldst steer thy ship through the dark billows, put the tiller into the hand of the Almighty. Many a rock might be escaped if we would let our Father take the helm; many a shoal or quicksand we might well avoid if we would leave it to His sovereign will to choose and to command. The Puritan said, "As sure as ever a Christian carves for himself he'll cut his own fingers." "I will instruct thee and teach thee in the way which thou shalt go," is God's promise to His people. Let us, then, take all our perplexities to Him and say, "Lord, what wilt thou have me to do?" Leave not thy chamber this morning without *enquiring of the Lord.* — *Spurgeon*

A certain man ... who never had walked ... heard Paul speak: who ... perceiving that he had faith to be healed, said ... Stand upright on thy feet. And he leaped and walked.

— Acts 14:8, 9, 10

Where true faith is, it will induce obedience; and where it does induce obedience, it will always, in one form or another, bring a blessing. — *W. Hay Aitken*

Then said Martha unto Jesus, Lord ... I know ... that whatso-

*ever thou wilt ask of God, God will give it thee. Jesus saith unto
her, Thy brother shall rise again. Martha saith unto Him, I know
that he shall rise again in the resurrection at the last day.*
— John 11:21, 22, 23, 24

Beware, in your prayer, above everything, of limiting God,
not only by unbelief, but by fancying that you know what He
can do. Expect unexpected things, *above all that* we ask or
think. Each time you intercede, be quiet first and worship God
in His glory. Think of what He can do, of how He delights to
hear Christ, of your place in Christ; and expect great things.
— *Andrew Murray*

*As many of you as have been baptized into Christ have put on
Christ.* — Gal. 3:27

.Not simply the righteousness of our Savior, not simply the
beauty of His holiness or the graces of His character, are we to
put on as a garment. The Lord Himself is our vesture. Every
Christian is not only a Christ-bearer but a Christ-wearer. We
are so to enter into Him by communion, to be so endured with
His presence, and embued with His Spirit that men shall see
Him when they behold us, as they see our garments when they
look upon our bodies. — *A. J. Gordon*

Thou shalt never wash my feet. — John 13:8

Whatever hinders us from receiving a blessing that God is
willing to bestow upon us is not humility, but the mockery of
it. A genuine humility will ever feel the need of the largest
measures of grace, and will be perfected just in the degree in
which that grace is bestowed. The truly humble man will seek
to be filled with all the fulness of God, knowing that when so
filled there is not the slightest place for pride or for self.
— *George Bowen*

Cast thy burden upon the Lord, and He shall sustain thee.
— Psa. 55:22

He that taketh his own cares upon himself loads himself with an uneasy burden. The fear of what *may* come, expectation of what *will* come, desire of what will *not* come, and the inability to redress all these, must needs bring him continual torment. I will cast my cares upon *God:* He hath bidden me. They cannot hurt Him: He can redress them. —*Hall*

Well done, good and faithful servant.... Thou wicked and slothful servant. — Matt. 25:21, 26

God holds us responsible not for what we *have,* but for what we *might have;* not for what we *are,* but for what we *might* be.
— *Mark Guy Pearse*

Jesus constrained His disicples to get into a ship. — Matt. 15:22

Jesus *constrained* them to go! One would think that if ever there was the certain promise of success in a mission, it was here. Surely, here, if anywhere, a triumphant issue might have been confidently predicted; and yet here, more than anywhere, there was seeming failure. He sent them out on a voyage, and they met such a storm as they had never yet experienced.

Let me ponder this, for it has been so with me, too. I have sometimes felt myself impelled to act by an influence which seemed above me — constrained to put to sea. The belief that I was constrained gave me confidence, and I was sure of a calm voyage. But the result was outward failure. The calm became a storm; the sea raged, the winds roared, the ship tossed in the midst of the waves, and my enterprise was wrecked ere it could reach the land.

Was, then, my divine command a delusion?

Nay; nor yet was my mission a failure. He did send me on that voyage, but He did not send me for *my* purpose. He had one end and I had another. My end was the outward calm; His was my meeting with the storm. My end was to gain the harbor of a material rest; His was to teach me there is a rest even on the open sea. — *George Matheson*

Study to shew theyself approved unto God, a workman that needeth not to be ashamed, rightly dividing the word of truth.

— II Tim. 2:15

Have thy tools ready; God will find thee work.

— *Charles Kinglsey*

Come out from among them, and be ye separate. — I Cor. 6:17

With all the world in his choice, God placed His ancient people in a very remarkable situation. On the north they were walled in by the snowy ranges of Lebanon; a barren desert formed their eastern boundary; far to the south stretched a sterile region, called the howling wilderness; while the sea — not then, as now, the highway of the nations, facilitating rather than impeding intercourse — lay on their west, breaking on a shore that had few harbors and no navigable rivers to invite the steps of commerce.

May we not find a great truth in the very position in which God placed His chosen people? It cetrainly teaches us that to be holy, or sanctified, we must be a separate people — living in the world, but not of it — as oil, that may be mixed, but cannot be combined with water. — *Guthrie*

I am with thee, and will keep thee in all places whither thou goest, and will bring thee again into this land. — Gen. 28:15

"With thee," companionship; "Keep thee," guardianship; "Bring thee," guidance.

I have set thee . . . that thou shouldst be for salvation unto the ends of the earth. — Acts 13:47
Ye shall be witnesses unto me . . . unto the uttermost parts of the earth. — Acts 1:8

Men are questioning now, as they never have questioned before, whether Christianity is, indeed, the true religion which is to be the salvation of the world. Christian men, it is for us to give our bit of answer to that question. It is for us, in whom the Christian church is at this moment partially embodied, to declare that Christianity, that the Christian faith, the Christian manhood can do that for the world which the world needs.

You ask, "What can I do?"

You can furnish one Chrisitan life. You can furnish a life so faithful to every duty, so ready for every service, so determined not to commit every sin, that the great Christian church shall be the stronger for your living in it, and the problem of the world be answered, and a certain great peace come into this poor, perplexed, phase of our humanity as it sees that new revelation of what Christianity is. — *Philips Brooks*

I know whom I have believed. — II Tim. 1:12

Personal acquaintance with Christ is a living thing. Like a tree that uses every hour for growth, it thrives in sunshine, it is refreshed by rain — even the storm drives it to fasten its grip more firmly in the earth for its support. So, troubled heart, in all experience, say, "This comes that I may make closer acquaintance with my Lord." — *Selected*

Wait for the promise of the Father. — Acts 1:4
When the day of Pentecost was fully come, they were all with one accord in one place...and they were all filled with the Holy Ghost. — Acts 2:1, 4

Obedience to a divine prompting transforms it into a permanent acquisition. — *F. B. Meyer*

We have known and believed the love that God hath to us.
                                                    — I John 4:16

The secret of walking closely with Christ, and working successfully for Him, is to fully realize that we are His beloved. Let us but feel that He has set His heart upon us, that He is watching us from those heavens with tender interest, that He is working out the mystery of our lives with solicitude and fondness, that He is following us day by day as a mother follows her babe in his first attempt to walk alone, that He has set His love upon us, and, in spite of ourselves, is working out for us His highest will and blessing, as far as we will let Him, and then nothing can discourage us. Our hearts will glow with responsive love. Our faith will spring to meet His mighty promises, and our sacrifices shall become the very luxuries of love for one so dear. This was the secret of John's spirit. "We have known and believed the love that God hath to us." And the heart that has fully learned this has found the secret of unbounded faith and enthusiastic service. — *A. B. Simpson*

Endure . . . as a good soldier of Jesus Christ. — II Tim. 2:3

Life is not victory, but battle. Be patient a little longer. By and by, each in his turn, we shall hear the sunset gun. — *Selected*

Whosoever doth not bear his cross and come after me, cannot be my disciple. — Luke 14:27

There is always the shadow of the cross resting upon the Christian's path. Is that a reason why you should avoid or not undertake the duty? Have you made up your mind that you will follow your Master everywhere else, save when he ascends the path that leads to the cross? Is that your religion? The sooner you change it, the better. The religion of the Lord Jesus Christ is the religion of the cross, and unless we take up our cross, we can never follow Him. — *W. Hay Aitken*

These . . . have turned the world upside down. — Acts 18:6

The serene beauty of a holy life is the most powerful influence in the world next to the might of God. — *Pascal*

What I do thou knowest not now; but thou shalt know hereafter. — John 13:7

God keeps a school for His children here on earth and one of His best teachers is Disappointment. My friend, when you and I reach our Father's house, we shall look back and see that the sharp-voiced, rough visaged teacher, Disappointment,

was one of the best guides to train us for it. He gave us hard lessons; he often used the rod; he often led us into thorny paths; he sometimes stripped off a load of luxuries; but that only made us travel the freer and the faster on our heaven-ward way. He sometimes led us down into the valley of the death shadow; but never did the promises read so sweetly as when spelled out by the eye of faith in that very valley. Nowhere did he lead us so often, or teach us such sacred lessons, as at the cross of Christ. Dear, old, rough-handed teacher! We will build a monument to thee yet, and crown it with garlands, and inscribe on it: *Blessed be the memory of Disappointment!*
— *Theodore Cuyler*

As thy days, so shall thy strength be. — Deut. 33:25
I can do all things through Christ which strengtheneth me.
— Phil. 4:13

He will not impose upon you one needless burden. He will not exact more than He knows your strength will bear. He will ask no Peter to come to Him on the water, unless He impart at the same time strength and support on the unstable waves. He will not ask you to draw water if the well is too deep, or to withdraw the stone if too heavy. But neither at the same time will He admit as an impossibility that which, as a free and responsible agent, it is in your power to avert. He will not regard as your misfortune what is your crime. — *Macduff*

Thy heart is not right in the sight of God. — Acts 8:21

The worst of all mockeries is a religion that leaves the heart unchanged: a religion that has *everything* but the love of Christ enshrined in the soul. — *F. Whitfield*

The Holy Ghost said, Separate me Barnabas and Saul for the work whereunto I have called them. — Acts 12:2

We have such a nice little quiet, shady corner in the vineyard, down among the tender grapes, with such easy little weedings and waterings to attend to. And then the Master comes and draws us out into the thick of the work, and puts us in a part of the field where we never should have thought of going, and puts larger tools into our hands, that we may do more at a stroke. And we know we are not sufficient for these things, and the very tools seem too heavy for us, and the glare too dazzling and the vines too tall. Ah! but would we dally, go back? He would not be in the shady corner with us now; for when He put us forth He went before us, and it is only by closely following that we can abide with Him.

— *Frances Ridley Havergal*

Small things. — Zech. 4:10

It is the little words you speak, the little thoughts you think, the little things you do or leave undone, the little moments you waste or use wisely, the little temptations which you yield to or overcome — the little things of every day that are making or marring your future life. — *Selected*

Be perfect, be of good comfort. — II Cor. 13:11

A glance at the words is enough to make us feel how contradictory they are. *Be perfect* — that is a word that strikes us with despair; at once we feel how faraway we are from our own poor ideal, and alas! how much further from God's ideal concerning us. *Be of good comfort* — ah, that is very different! That seems to say, "Do not fret; do not fear. If you are not what you would be, you must be thankful for what you are."

Now the question is this — How can these two be reconciled?

It is only the religion of Jesus Christ that reconciles them. He stands in our midst, and with the right hand of His righteousness He pointeth us upward, and saith, "Be perfect." There is no resting place short of that. Yet with the left hand of His love He doth encompass us, as He saith, "Soul, be of good comfort; for that is what I came to do for thee."

— *Mark Guy Pearse*

Be ye therefore perfect, even as your Father which is in heaven is perfect. — Matt. 5:48

Seeking the aid of the Holy Spirit, let us aim at perfection. Let every day see some sin crucified, some battle fought, some good done, some victory won; let every fall be followed by a rise, and every step gained become, not a resting-place, but a new starting-point for further and higher progress. — *Guthrie*

Sleep on now, and take your rest. — Mark 14:41

Never did that sacred opportunity to watch with Christ return to His disciples. Lost then, it was lost forever. And now when Jesus is still beholding the travail of His soul in the redemption of the world, if you fail to be with Him watching for souls as they that must give account, remember that the opportunity will never return. "Watch, therefore," says your Lord, "lest coming suddenly, He may find you sleeping."

— *A. J. Gordon*

Let us not sleep, as do others. — I Thess. 5:6

There are many ways of promoting Christian wakefulness. Among the rest, let me strongly advise Christians to converse together concerning the ways of the Lord. Christian and Hopeful, as they journeyed towards the Celestial City, said to themselves:

"To prevent drowsiness in this place, let us fall into good discourse."

Christians who isolate themselves and walk alone are very liable to grow drowsy. Hold Christian company, and you will be kept wakeful by it, and refreshed and encouraged to make quicker progress in the road to heaven. — *Spurgeon*

ILLUSTRATIONS

LADY PENDULUM

W<small>HEN</small> M<small>R</small>. S<small>ANKEY</small> and I were in London a lady who attended our meetings was brought into the house in her carriage, being unable to walk. At first she was very skeptical; but one day she said to her servant:

"Take me into the inquiry room."

After I had talked with her a good while about her soul she said:

"But you will go back to America, and it will be all over."

"Oh, no," said I, "it is going to last forever."

I couldn't make her believe it. I don't know how many times I talked with her. At last I used the fable of the pendulum in the clock. The pendulum figured up the thousands of times it would have to tick, and got discouraged, and was going to give up. Then it thought, "It is only a tick at a time," and went on. So it is in the Christian life — only one step at a time. That helped this lady very much. She began to see that if she could trust in God for a supply of grace for only one day, she could go right on in the same way from day to day. As soon as she saw this, she came out quite decided. But she never could get done talking about that pendulum. The servants called her Lady Pendulum. She had a pendulum put up in her room to remind her of the illustration, and when I went away from London she gave me a clock — I've got it in my house still.

THE GREATER MYSTERY

Dr. Andrew Bonar once said that, although it was a mystery to him how sin should have come into the world, it was still a greater mystery how God should have come here to bear the penalty of it Himself.

NEVER RUNS DRY

I remember being in a city where I noticed that the people resorted to a favorite well in one of the parks. I said to a man one day:

"Does the well never run dry?"

The man was drinking of the water out of the well; and as he stopped drinking, he smacked his lips and said:

"They have never been able to pump it dry yet. They tried it a few years ago. They put the fire-engines to work, and tried all they could to pump the well dry; but they found there was a river flowing right under the city."

Thank God, the well of salvation can never run dry either!

HE TRUSTED HIS FATHER

A party of gentlemen in Scotland wanted to get some eggs from a nest on the side of a precipice, and they tried to persuade a poor boy that lived near to go over and get them, saying they would hold him by a rope. They offered him a good deal of money; but they were strangers to him, and he would not go. They told him they would see that no accident happened to him; they would hold the rope.

At last he said: "I will go if my father will hold the rope." He trusted his father.

A man will not trust strangers. I want to get acquainted with a man before I put my confidence in him. I have known God for forty years, and I have more confidence in Him now than I ever had before; it increases every year.

PEACE DECLARED

When France and England were at war once a French vessel

had gone off on a long whaling voyage. When they came back, the crew were short of water, and being near an English port, they wanted to get water; but they were afraid that they would be taken prisoners if they went into that port. Some people in the port saw their signal of distress, and sent word that they need not be afraid, that the war was over, and peace had been declared. But they couldn't make those sailors believe it, and they didn't dare to go into port, although they were out of water. At last they made up their minds that they had better go in and surrender their cargo and their lives to their enemies rather than perish at sea without water; and when they got in, they found out that what had been told them was true, that peace had been declared.

There are a great many people who don't believe the glad tidings that peace has been made by Jesus Christ between God and man, but it is true.

SAWDUST OR BREAD

If you go out to your garden and throw down some sawdust, the birds will not take any notice; but if you throw down some crumbs, you will find they will soon sweep down and pick them up.

The true child of God can tell the difference (so to speak) between sawdust and bread. Many so-called Christians are living on the world's sawdust, instead of being nourished by the Bread that cometh down from heaven. Nothing can satisfy the longings of the soul but the Word of the living God.

"BABY'S FEEDING HIMSELF!"

You know it is always regarded a great event in the family when a child can feed itself. It is propped up at table, and at first perhaps it uses the spoon upside down, but by and by it uses it all right, and mother, or perhaps sister, claps her hands and says:

"Just see, baby's feeding himself!"

Well, what we need as Christians is to be able to feed ourselves. How many there are who sit helpless and listless, with open mouths, hungry for spiritual things, and the minister has to try to feed them, while the Bible is a feast prepared, into which they never venture.

SHOULD NOT BE POSTPONED

In 1871 I preached a series of sermons on the life of Christ in old Farwell hall, Chicago, for five nights. I took Him from the cradle and followed Him up to the judgment hall, and on that occasion I consider I made as great a blunder as ever I made in my life. It was upon that memorable night in October, and the court-house bell was sounding an alarm of fire, but I paid no attention to it. You know we were accustomed to hear the fire-bell often, and it didn't disturb us much when it sounded. I finished the sermon upon "What Shall I Do with Jesus?" and said to the audience:

"Now, I want you to take the question with you and think it over, and next Sunday I want you to come back and tell me what you are going to do with Him."

What a mistake! It seems now as if Satan was in my mind when I said this. Since then I never have dared give an audience a week to think of their salvation. If they were lost, they might rise up in judgment against me. "Now is the accepted time."

I remember Mr. Sankey singing, and how his voice rang when he came to that pleading verse:

> "To-day the Savior calls,
> For refuge fly!
> The storm of Justice falls,
> And death is nigh!"

After the meeting we went home. I remember going down La Salle street with a young man, and saw the glare of flames. I said to the young man:

"This means ruin to Chicago."

About one o'clock Farwell hall was burned; soon the church in which I had preached went down, and everything was scattered. I never saw that audience again.

My friends, we don't know what may happen to-morrow, but there is one thing I do know, and that is, if you take the gift of God you are saved. If you have eternal life you need not fear fire, death, or sickness. Let disease or death come, you can shout triumphantly over the grave if you have Christ. My friends, what are you going to do with Him? Will you not decide now?

ANECDOTES

W<small>HEN</small> I <small>WAS</small> preaching in Baltimore in 1879, an infidel reporter, who believed I was a humbug, came to the meetings with the express purpose of catching me in my remarks. He believed that my stories and anecdotes were all made up, and he intended to expose me in his paper.

One of the anecdotes I told was as follows:

A gentleman was walking down the streets of a city some time before. It was near Christmas-time, and many of the shop windows were filled with Christmas presents and toys. As this gentleman passed along, he saw three little girls standing before a shop window. Two of them were trying to describe to the third the things that were in the window. It aroused his attention, and he wondered what it could mean. He went back, and found that the middle one was blind — she had never been able to see — and her two sisters were endeavoring to tell her how the things looked. The gentleman stood beside them for some time and listened; he said it was most interesting to hear them trying to describe the different articles to the blind child — they found it a difficult task.

"That is just my position in trying to tell other men about Christ," I said; "I may talk about Him; and yet they see no beauty in Him that they should desire Him. But if they will only come to Him, He will open their eyes and reveal Himself to them in all His loveliness and grace."

After the meeting this reporter came to me and asked where

I got that story. I said I had read it in a Boston paper. He told me that it had happened right there in the streets of Baltimore, and that he was the gentleman referred to! It made such an impression on him that he accepted Christ and became one of the first converts in that city.

Many and many a time I have found that when the sermon — and even the text — has been forgotten, some story has fastened itself in a hearer's mind, and has borne fruit. Anecdotes are like windows to let light in upon a subject. They have a useful ministry, and I pray God to bless this collection to every reader.

WANTED – A NEW SONG!

There was a Wesleyan preacher in England, Peter Mackenzie, full of native humor, a most godly man. He was once preaching from the text: "And They Sang a New Song," and he said:

"Yes, there will be singing in heaven, and when I get there I will want to have David with his harp, and Paul, and Peter and other saints gather around for a sing. And I will announce a hymn from the Wesleyan Hymnal. 'Let us sing hymn No. 749 –'

My God, my Father, while I stray —

"But some one will say, 'That won't do. You are in heaven, Peter; there's no straying here.' And I will say, 'Yes, that's so. Let us sing No. 651 –'

Though waves and storms go o'er my head,

Though friends be gone and hopes be dead —

"But another saint will interrupt, 'Peter, you forget you are in heaven now; there are no storms here.' 'Well, I will try again, No. 536 –'

Into a world of ruffians sent —

" 'Peter! Peter!' some one will say, 'we will put you out unless you stop giving out inappropriate hymns.' I will ask — what can we sing? And they will all say:

" 'Sing the new song, the song of Moses and the Lamb.' "

NOTHING TO HOLD ON TO

It is related of an atheist who was dying that he appeared very uncomfortable, very unhappy and frightened. Another atheist who stood at his bedside said to him:

"Don't be afraid. Hold on, man, hold on to the last."

The dying man said: "That is what I want to do, but tell me what to hold on to?"

WHAT COULD THE KING DO?

In the second century they brought a Christian before a king, who wanted him to recant and give up Christ and Christianity, but the man spurned the proposition. But the king said:

"If you don't do it, I will banish you."

The man smiled and answered, "You can't banish me from Christ, for He says He will never leave me nor forsake me."

The king got angry, and said: "Well, I will confiscate your property and take it all from you."

And the man replied: "My treasures are laid up on high; you cannot get them."

The king became still more angry, and said: "I will kill you."

"Why," the man answered, "I have been dead forty years; I have been dead with Christ, dead to the world, and my life is hid with Christ in God, and you cannot touch it."

"What are you going to do with such a fanatic? said the king.

ALWAYS PRAISING

A man was converted some years ago, and he was just full of praise. He was living in the light all the time. He used to preface everything he said in the meeting with "Praise God!"

One night he came to the meeting with his finger all bound up. He had cut it, and cut it pretty bad, too. Well, I wondered how he would praise God for this; but he got up and said:

"I have cut my finger, but, praise God, I didn't cut it off!"

If things go against you, just remember they might be a good deal worse.

NOT AT ALL ABSURD

A man said to me some time ago, "Moody, the doctrine you preach is most absurd: you preach that men have only to *believe* to change the whole course of their life. A man will not change his course by simply believing."

I said — "I think I can make you believe that in less than two minutes."

"No, you can't" he said; "I'll never believe it."

I said, "Let us make sure that we understand each other. You say a man is not affected by what he believes, that it will not change the course of his actions?"

"I do."

"Supposing," I said "a man should put his head in at that door and say the house was on fire, what would you do? You would get out by the window if you believed it wouldn't you?"

"Oh," he replied, "I didn't think of that!"

"No," I said, "I guess you didn't."

Belief is the foundation of all society, of commerce, and of everything else.

WORD STUDY

Another way to study the Bible is to take one word and follow it up with the help of a concordance.

Or take just one word that runs through a book. Some time ago I was wonderfully blessed by taking the seven *"Blesseds"* of the Revelation. If God did not wish us to understand the book of Revelation, He would not have given it to us at all. A good many say it is so dark and mysterious that common readers cannot understand it. Let us only keep digging away at it, and it will unfold itself by and by. Some one says it is the only book in the Bible that tells about the devil being chained; and as the devil knows that, he goes up and down Christendom and says, "It is no use your reading Revelation, you can not understand the book; it is too hard for you." The fact is, he does not want you to understand about his own defeat. Just look at the *blessings* the book contains:

1. *"Blessed is* he that readeth, and they that hear the words of this prophecy, and keep those things which are written therein: for the time is at hand."

2. *"Blessed* are the dead which die in the Lord. . . . Yea, saith the Spirit, that they may rest from their labors."

3. *"Blessed* is he that watcheth and keepeth his garments."

4. *"Blessed* are they which are called to the marriage supper of the Lamb."

5. *"Blessed* and holy is he that hath part in the first resurrection. On such the second death hath no power; but they

shall be priests of God and of Christ, and shall reign with him a thousand years."

6. *"Blessed* is he that keepeth the sayings of the prophecy of this book."

7. *"Blessed* are they that do His commandments, that they may have right to the tree of life, and may enter in through the gates into the city."

Or you may take the eight *"overcomes"* in Revelation; and you will be wonderfully blessed by them. They take you right up to the throne of heaven; you climb by them to the throne of God.

I have been greatly blessed by going through the *"believings"* of John. Every chapter but two speaks of believing. As I said before, he wrote his gospel that we might believe. All through it is "Believe! *Believe!"* If you want to persuade a man that Christ is the Son of God, John's gospel is the book for him.

Take the six *"precious"* things in Peter's Epistles. And the seven *"walks"* of the Epistle to the Ephesians. And the five *"much mores"* of Romans 5. Or the two *"received"* of John 1. Or the seven *"hearts"* in Proverbs 23, and especially an eighth. Or *"the fear of the Lord"* in Proverbs: —

"The fear of the Lord is the beginning of wisdom.

"The fear of the Lord is to hate evil.

"The fear of the Lord prolongeth days.

"In *the fear of the Lord* is strong confidence.

"The fear of the Lord is a fountain of Life.

"Better is little with the *fear of the Lord* than great treasure and trouble therewith.

"The fear of the Lord is the instruction of wisdom.

"By *the fear of the Lord* men depart from evil.

"The fear of the Lord tendeth to life.

"By humility and *the fear of the Lord* are riches and honor and life.

"Be thou in *the fear of the Lord* all the day long."

KEY WORDS

A friend gave me some key words recently. He said Peter wrote about *Hope:* "When the Chief Shepherd shall appear." The keynote of Paul's writings seemed to be *Faith,* and that of John's, *Love.* "Faith, hope and charity," these were the characteristics of the three men, the key-notes to the whole of their teachings. James wrote of *Good Works,* and Jude of *Apostasy.*

In the general epistles of Paul some one suggested the phrase *"in Christ."* In the book of Romans we find justification by faith *in Christ.* Corinthians presents sanctification *in Christ.* The book of Galatians, adoption or liberty *in Christ.* Ephesians presents fulness *in Christ.* Philippians, consolation *in Christ.* In Colossians we have completeness *in Christ.* Thessalonians gives us hope *in Christ.*

Different systems of key words are published by Bible scholars, and it is a good thing for every one to know one system or other.

BIBLE MARKING

D ON'T BE AFRAID to borrow and lend Bibles. Some time ago
a man wanted to take my Bible home to get a few things out
of it, and when it came back I found this noted in it:

Justification, a change of state, a new standing before God.

Repentance, a change of mind, a new mind about God.

Conversion, a change of life, a new life for God.

Adoption, a change of family, new relationship towards God.

Sanctification, a change of service, separation unto God.

Glorification, a new state, a new condition with God.

In the same hand-writing I found these lines:

Jesus only; the light of heaven is the face of Jesus.

The joy of heaven is the presence of Jesus.

The melody of heaven is the name of Jesus.

The theme of heaven is the work of Jesus.

The employment of heaven is the service of Jesus.

The fulness of heaven is Jesus Himself.

The duration of heaven is the eternity of Jesus.

BIBLE MARKING: ITS NECESSITY

An old writer said that some books are to be tasted, some
to be swallowed, and some to be chewed and digested. The Bible
is one that you can never exhaust. It is like a bottomless well:
you can always find fresh truths gushing forth from its pages.

Hence the great fascination of constant and earnest Bible
study. Hence also the necessity of marking your Bible. Unless
you have an uncommon memory, you cannot retain the good

things you hear. If you trust to your ear alone, they will escape you in a day or two; but if you mark your Bible and enlist the aid of your eye, you will never lose them. The same applies to what you read.

ITS ADVANTAGES

Bible marking should be made the servant of the memory. If properly done, it sharpens the memory, rather than blunts it, because it gives prominence to certain things that catch the eye, which by constant reading you get to learn off by heart.

It helps you to locate texts.

It saves you the trouble of writing out notes of your addresses. Once in the margin, always ready.

I have carried one Bible with me a great many years. It is worth a good deal to me, and I will tell you why; because I have so many passages marked in it, that if I am called upon to speak at any time I am ready. I have little words marked in the margin, and they are a sermon to me. Whether I speak about *Faith, Hope, Charity, Assurance,* or any subject whatever, it all comes back to me; and however unexpectedly I am called upon to preach, I am always ready. Every child of God ought to be like a soldier, and always hold himself in readiness. If the Queen of England's army were ordered to India tomorrow, the soldier is ready for the journey. But we can not be ready if we do not study the Bible. So whenever you hear a good thing, just put it down, because if it is good for you it will be good for somebody else; and we should pass the coin of heaven around just as we do the coin of the realm.

People tell me they have nothing to say. "Out of the abundance of the heart, the mouth speaketh." Get full of Scripture and then you can't help but say it. It says itself. Keep the world out of your heart by getting full of something else. A man tried to build a flying machine. He made some wings and filled them with gas. He said he couldn't quite fly, but that he was lighter than the air and it helped him over lots of obstructions. So when you get these heavenly truths, they are lighter than the air down here and help you over trouble.

Bible marking makes the Bible a new book to you. If there was a white birch tree within a quarter of a mile of the home of your boyhood, you would remember it all your life. Mark your Bible, and instead of its being dry and uninteresting, it will become a beautiful book to you. What you see makes a more lasting impression on your memory than what you hear.

HOW TO MARK AND WHAT TO MARK

There are many methods of marking. Some use six or eight colored inks or pencils. Black is used to mark texts that refer to sin; red, all references to the cross; blue, all references to heaven; and so on. Others invent symbols. When there is any reference to the cross, they put "†" in the margin. Some write "G", meaning the Gospel.

There is danger of overdoing this and making your marks more prominent than the scripture itself. If the system is complicated it becomes a burden, and you are likely to get confused. It is easier to remember the text than the meaning of your marks.

Black ink is good enough for all purposes. I use no other, unless it be red ink to draw attention to "the blood."

The simplest way to mark is to underline the words or to make a stroke alongside the verse. Another good way is to go over the printed letters with your pen, and make them thicker. The word will then stand out like heavier type. Mark "only" in Psalm 62 in this way.

When any word or phrase is oft repeated in a chapter or book, put consecutive numbers in the margin over against the text. Thus, in the second chapter of Habakkuk, we find five "woes" against five common sins; (1) verse 6, (2) verse 9, (3) verse 12, (4) verse 15, (5) verse 19. Number the ten plagues in this way. When there is a succession of promises or charges in a verse, it is better to write the numbers small at the beginning of each separate promise. Thus, there is a seven-fold promise to Abraham in Gen. 12:2-3; "(1) I will make of thee a great nation, (2) and I will bless thee, (3) and make thy name great; (4) and thou shalt be a blessing; (5) and I will bless them that bless thee, (6) and curse him that curseth thee: (7) and in thee shall all families of the earth be blessed." In Prov. 1:22, we have (1) simple ones, (2) scorners, (3) fools.

Put a "x" in the margin against things not generally observed: for example, the laws regarding women wearing men's clothes, and regarding bird-nesting, in Deut. 22:5-6; the sleep of the poor man and of the rich man compared, Ecc. 5:12.

I also find it helpful to mark: 1. cross-references. Opposite Gen. 1:1, write "Through faith, Heb. 11:3" — because there we read — "Through faith we understand that the words were framed by the word of God." Opposite Gen. 28:12, write — "An answer to prayer, Gen. 35:3." Opposite Matt. 6:33, write "I Kings 3:13" and "Luke 10:42," which give illustrations of seeking the kingdom of God first. Opposite Gen. 37:7, write — "Gen. 50:18" — which is the fulfilment of the dream.

2. Railroad connections, that is, connections made by fine lines running across the page. In Daniel 6, connect "will deliver" (v. 16), "able to deliver" (v. 20), and "hath delivered" (v. 5) with "come and hear" (v. 16).

3. Variations of the Revised Version: thus Romans 8:26 reads — "the Spirit Himself" in the R. V., not "itself." Note also marginal readings like Mark 6:19, "an inward grudge" instead of "a quarrel."

4. Words that have changed their meaning; "meal" for "meat" in Leviticus. Or where you can explain a difficulty: "above" for "upon" in Num. 11:31. Or where the English does not bring out the full meaning of the original as happens in the names

of God: "Elohim" in Gen. 1:1, "Jehovah Elohim" in Gen. 2:4, "El Shaddai" in Gen. 17:1, and so on.

5. Unfortunate divisions of chapters. The last verse of John 7 reads — "And every man went unto his own house." Chapter 8 begins "Jesus went unto the mount of Olives." There ought to be no division of chapters here.

6. At the beginning of every book write a short summary of its contents, something like the summary given in some Bibles at the head of every chapter.

7. Key words and key verses.

8. Make a note of any text that marks a religious crisis in your life. I once heard Rev. F. B. Meyer preach on I Cor. 1:9, and he asked his hearers to write on their Bibles that they were that day "called unto the fellowship of His Son Christ our Lord."

TAKING NOTES

When a preacher gives out a text, mark it; as he goes on preaching, put a few words in the margin, key-words that shall bring back the whole sermon again. By that plan of making a few marginal notes, I can remember sermons I heard years and years ago. Every man ought to take down some of the preacher's words and ideas, and go into some lane or by-way, and preach them again to others. We ought to have four ears — two for ourselves and two for other people. Then, if you are in a new town, and have nothing else to say, jump up and say: "I heard someone say so and so"; and men will always be glad to hear you if you give them heavenly food. The world is perishing for lack of it.

Some years ago I heard an Englishman in Chicago preach from a curious text: "There be four things which are little upon the earth, but they are exceeding wise." "Well," said I to myself, "what will you make of these 'little things'? I have seen them a good many times." Then he went on speaking: "The ants are a people not strong, yet they prepare their meat in the summer."

He said God's people are like the ants. "Well," I thought, "I have seen a good many of them, but I never saw one like me." "They are like the ants," he said, "because they are laying up treasure in heaven, and preparing for the future; but the world rushes madly on, and forgets all about God's command to lay up for ourselves incorruptible treasures."

"The conies are but a feeble folk, yet make these their houses in the rocks." He said, "The conies are very weak things; if you were to throw a stick at one of them you could kill it; but they are very wise, for they build their houses in rocks, where they are out of harm's way. And God's people are very wise, although very feeble; for they build on the Rock of Ages, and that Rock is Christ." "Well," I said, "I am certainly like the conies."

Then came the next verse: "The locusts have no king, yet go they forth all of them by bands." I wondered what he was going to make of that. "Now God's people," he said, "have no king down here. The world said, 'Caesar is our king'; but he is not *our* King; our King is the Lord of Hosts. The locusts went out by bands; so do God's people. Here is a Presbyterian band, here an Episcopalian band, here a Methodist band, and so on; but by and by the great King will come and catch up all these separate bands, and they will all be one; one fold and one Shepherd." And when I heard that explanation, I said; "I would be like the locusts." I have become so sick, my friends, of this miserable sectarianism, that I wish it could all be swept away.

"Well," he went on again, "the spider taketh hold with her hands, and is in kings' palaces." When he got to the spider, I said, "I don't like that at all; I don't like the idea of being compared to a spider." "But," he said, "If you go into a king's palace, there is the spider hanging on his gossamer web, and looking down with scorn and contempt on the gilded salon; he is laying hold of things above. And so every child of God ought to be like the spider, and lay hold of the unseen things of God.

You see, then, my brethren, we who are God's people are like the ants, the conies, the locusts, and the spiders, little things, but exceeding wise." I put that down in the margin of my Bible, and the recollection of it does me as much good now as when I first heard it.

A friend of mine was in Edinburgh and he heard one of the leading Scotch Presbyterian ministers. He had been preaching from the text, "Every Eye shall see Him," and he closed up by saying: "Yes, every eye. Adam will see Him, and when he does he will say: 'This is He who was promised to me in that dark day when I fell; Abraham will see Him and will say: 'This is He whom I saw afar off; but now face to face'; Mary will see Him, and she will sing with new interest that magnificat. And I, too, shall see Him, and when I do, I will sing: 'Rock of Ages, cleft for me, Let me hide myself in Thee.'"

ADDITIONAL EXAMPLES

Turn to Exodus 6:6, 7, 8. In these verses we find seven "I wills."

I will bring you out from under the burden of the Egyptians.

I will rid you out of their bondage.

I will redeem you with a stretched-out arm.

I will be to you a God.

I will bring you in unto the land [of Canaan].

I will give it to you for a heritage.

Again: Isaiah 41:10. "Fear thou not, for I am with thee; be not dismayed, for I am thy God; I will strengthen thee; yea, I will help thee; yea, I will uphold thee with the right hand of my righteousness." Mark what God says:

He is *with* His servant.

He is his *God*.

He will *strengthen*.

He will *help*.

He will *uphold*.

Again: Psalm 103:2: "Bless the Lord, O my soul, and forget not all his benefits." If you can not remember them all, remember what you can. In the next three verses there are five things:

Who *forgiveth* all thine iniquities.

Who *healeth* all thy diseases.

Who *redeemeth* thy life from destruction.

Who *crowneth* thee with loving kindness and tender mercies.

Who *satisfieth* thy mouth with good things.

We can learn some things about the mercy of the Lord from this same Psalm:

v. 4 — Its quality, "tender."

v. 8 — Its measure, "plenteous."

v. 11 — Its magnitude, "great," "according to the height of the heaven above the earth." See margin.

v. 17 — Its duration, "from everlasting to everlasting."

Twenty-third Psalm. I suppose I have heard as many good sermons on the twenty-third Psalm as on any other six verses in the Bible. I wish I had begun to take notes upon them years ago when I heard the first one. Things slip away from you when you get to be fifty years of age. Young men had better go into training at once.

With me, the Lord.

Beneath me, green pastures.

Beside me, still waters.

Before me, a table.

Around me, mine enemies.

After me, goodness and mercy.

Ahead of me, the house of the Lord.

"Blessed is the day," says an old divine, "when Psalm twenty-three was born!" It has been more used than almost any other passage in the Bible.

v. 1 — A happy life.

v. 4 — A happy death.

v. 6 — A happy eternity.

Take Psalm 102:6-7: "I am like a pelican of the wilderness; I am like an owl of the desert. I watch and am as a sparrow alone upon the housetop." It seems strange until you reflect that a pelican carries its food with it, that the owl keeps its eyes open at night, and that the sparrow watches alone. So the Christian must carry his food with him — the Bible — and he must keep his eyes open and watch alone.

Turn to Isaiah 32, and mark four things that God promises in verse 2: "And a man shall be as an hiding place from the wind, and a covert from the tempest; as rivers of water in a dry place, as the shadow of a great rock in a weary land." There we have: —

The hiding place from danger.

The cover from the tempest.

Rivers of water.

The Rock of Ages.

In the third and fourth verses of the same chapter: "And the eyes of them that see shall not be dim, and the ears of them that hear shall hearken. The heart also of the rash shall understand knowledge, and the tongue of the stammerers shall be ready to speak plainly." We have eyes, ears, heart and tongue, all ready to pay homage to the King of Righteousness.

Now turn into the New Testament, John 4:47-53.

The noble *heard* about Jesus.

> *went* unto Him.
> *besought* Him.
> *believed* Him.
> *knew* that his prayer was answered.

Again: Matthew 11:28-30:

"Come unto me, all ye that labour and are heavy-laden, and I will give you rest. Take my yoke upon you and learn of me; for I am meek and lowly in heart; and ye shall find rest unto your souls. For my yoke is easy, and my burden is light."

Someone has said these verses contain the only description we have of Christ's heart.

Something to do, come unto Jesus.

Something to leave, your burden.

Something to take, His yoke.

Something to find, rest unto your soul.

Again: John 14:6: "I am the way, the truth, and the life."

The way, follow me.

The truth, learn of me.

The life, abide in me.

SUGGESTIONS

Do not buy a Bible that you are unwilling to mark and use. An interleaved Bible gives more room for notes.

Be precise and concise: for example, Neh. 13:18: "A warning from history."

Never mark anything because you saw it in some one else's Bible. If it does not come home to you, if you do not understand it, do not put it down.

Never pass a nugget by without trying to grasp it. Then mark it down.

This was the last address delivered by D. L.
Moody on Round Top, where his body now
lies awaiting the resurrection

THE NINETY-FIRST PSALM

THIS PSALM might have been written by Moses after some terrible calamity had come upon the children of Israel. It might have been after that terrible night of death in Egypt, when the first-born from the palace to the hovel were slain; or after that terrible plague of fiery serpents in the wilderness, when the people were full of fear and in a nervous state. In the Western states, where they have terrible cyclones, the people, old and young, get very nervous, and whenever they see a cloud coming up, they are alarmed. I was in Iowa some time ago, after they had had in that state seven cyclones, one right after another. They had been all around the city that I was in, and if a storm came up and the black clouds began to gather, the whole city was just trembling.

Perhaps Moses called Aaron and Miriam, and Joshua and Caleb, and a few others into his tent and read this psalm to them first. How sweet it must have sounded, and how strange!

I can imagine Moses asking, "Do you think that will help them? Will that quiet them?" and they all thought that it would. And then (it may be), on one of those hill-tops of Sinai, at twilight, this psalm was read. How it must have soothed them, how it must have helped them, how it must have strengthened them!

You will notice in the last two verses there are seven things that God told Moses He would do, seven "I wills." If they could get burned down into our souls, it would be a help to us all through life. When God says He will do a thing, there is no power on earth or in perdition that can keep Him from doing that which He has promised to do.

1. *"I will deliver."*

First, "I will deliver." When God called Moses to go down into Egypt to deliver the children of Israel from the hand of the Egyptians, in all the world there wasn't a man who, humanly speaking, was less qualified than Moses. He had made the attempt once before to deliver the children of Israel, and he began by delivering one man. He failed in that, and killed an Egyptian, and had to run off into the desert, and stay there forty years. He had tried to deliver the Hebrews in his own way, he was working in his own strength and doing it in the energy of the flesh. He had all the wisdom of the Egyptians, but that didn't help him. He had to be taken back into Horeb, and kept there forty years in the school of God, before God could trust him to deliver the children of Israel in God's way. Then God came to him and said, "I have come down to deliver," and when God worked through Moses three million were delivered as easy as I can turn my hand over. God could do it. It was no trouble when God came on the scene.

Learn the lesson. If we want to be delivered, from every inward and outward foe, we must look to a higher source than ourselves. We cannot do it in our own strength.

We all have some weak point in our character. When we would go forward, it drags us back, and when we would rise up into higher spheres of usefulness and the atmosphere of heaven, something drags us down. Now I have no sympathy with the idea that God puts us behind the blood and saves us, and then leaves us in Egypt to be under the old taskmaster. I believe

God brings us out of Egypt into the promised land, and that it is the privilege of every child of God to be delivered from every foe, from every besetting sin.

If there is some sin that is getting the mastery over you, you certainly cannot be useful. You certainly cannot bring forth fruit to the honor and glory of God until you get self-control. "He that ruleth his spirit is better than he that taketh a city." If we haven't got victory over jealousy and worldly amusements and worldly pleasure, if we are not delivered from all these things, we are not going to have power with God or with men, and we are not going to be as useful as we might be if we got deliverance from every evil. There isn't an evil within or without but what He will deliver us from if we will let Him. That is what He wants to do. As God said to Moses, "I have come down to deliver." If He could deliver three million slaves from the hands of the mightiest monarch on earth, don't you think He can deliver us from every besetting sin, and give us complete victory over ourselves, over our temper, over our dispositions, over our irritableness and peevishness and snappishness? If we want it and desire it above everything else, we can get victory.

People are apt to think that these little things (as we call them) are weaknesses that we are not responsible for; that they are misfortunes, that we inherited them. I have heard people talk about their temper. They say,

"Well, I inherited it from my father and mother; they were quick-tempered, and I got it from them."

Well, that is a poor place to hide, my friend. Grace ought to deliver us from all those things.

A lady came to me some time ago and said she had great trouble with her temper now, and she was more irritable than she was five years ago, and she wanted to know if I didn't think it was wrong.

I said, "I should think you are backsliding. If you haven't

better control over yourself now than you had five years ago, there is something radically wrong."

"Well," she said, "I should like to know how I am going to mend it. Can you tell me?"

"Yes."

"How?"

I said, "When you get angry with people and give them a good scolding, go right to them after you have made up your mind that you have done wrong, and tell them you have sinned and ask them to forgive you."

She said she wouldn't like to do that.

Of course she wouldn't; but she will never get victory until she treats it as sin. Don't look upon it as weakness or misfortune, but sin. No child of God ought to lose control of temper without confessing it.

A lady came to me some time ago and said that she had got so in the habit of exaggerating that people accused her of misrepresentation. She wanted to know if there was any way she could overcome it.

"Certainly," I said.

"How?"

"Next time you catch yourself at it, go right to the party and tell them you lied."

"Oh!" she said, "I wouldn't call it lying."

Of course not, but a lie is a lie all the same, and you will never overcome those sins until you treat them as sins and get them out of your nature. If you want to shine in the light of God and be useful, you must overcome, you must be delivered. And that is what God says He will do; He will deliver.

II. *"I will answer."*

Now, the next "I will": — "He shall call upon me, and I will answer him."

There is a chance for all of us to call. The great God that

made heaven and earth has promised, "I will answer his call."
If you call on God for deliverance and for victory over sin and
every evil, God isn't going to turn a deaf ear to your call. I
don't care how black your life has been, I don't care what your
past record has been, I don't care how disobedient you have
been, I don't care how you have back-slidden and wandered;
if you really want to come back, God accepts the willing mind,
God will hear your prayer, and answer.

Listen to the prodigal: "Father, I have sinned!" That was
enough; the father took him right to his bosom. The past was
blotted out at once. Look at the men on the day of Pentecost.
Their hands were dripping with the blood of the Son of God;
they had murdered Jesus Christ. And what did Peter say to
them? "It shall come to pass, that whosoever shall call on the
name of the Lord shall be saved." Look at the penitent thief.
It might have been that when a little boy, his mother taught
him that same passage in Joel, "It shall come to pass, that whosoever shall call on the name of the Lord shall be saved." As
he hung there on the cross, it flashed into his mind that this
was the Lord of glory, and though he was on the very borders
of hell, he cried out, "Lord, remember me," and the answer came
right then and there, "This day thou shalt be with Me in
paradise." In the morning associated with thieves; in the evening, associated with the purest of heaven. In the morning,
cursing — Matthew and Mark both tell us that those two thieves
came out cursing; in the evening, uplifted on high, an inhabi-
tant of heaven. In the morning, as black as hell could make
him; in the evening, not a spot or wrinkle. Why? Because he
took God at His word.

My dear friend, if you are unsaved, you just call upon God
now, and here is a promise, "I will answer his call."

A few years ago an old returned missionary went to one of
our leading hospitals to have a surgical operation performed.
He was to go under ether, and it was doubtful whether he

would come out or not; he might wake up in another world. He bade adieu to his friends, gave them his farewell blessing — he was a very godly man — and when the doctor said, "Well, we are ready," he faced them, and with a calm look, he said:

"Would you just wait a minute?"

Then he lifted his voice in prayer —

> "Now I lay me down to sleep,
> I pray the Lord my soul to keep.
> If I should die before I wake,
> I pray the Lord my soul to take."

Then, opening his eyes, he said, "Doctor, I am ready," and passed under the knife, and out from under it into health.

My dear friends, it is a sweet privilege to pray; it is a sweet privilege to be in touch with heaven, to be in communion with the great God that made heaven and earth. "I will answer his call."

I suppose there isn't a Christian in this audience but can say Amen to that. You can say God has answered in the past, and you believe He will do so again.

Some people say they can't call. Perhaps you cannot make an eloquent prayer — I hope you can't — I have heard about all the eloquent prayers I want to. But you can say, "God, be merciful to me, a sinner."

Only be sincere, and God will hear your cry. Mark you, there is a sham cry. Mothers understand that; they know when their children cry in earnest, or whether it is a sham cry. Let the child give a real cry of distress, and the mother will leave every-thing and fly to her child. I have been forty years in Christian work, and I have never known God to disappoint any man or woman who was in earnest about their soul's salvation. I know lots of people who pretend to be in earnest, but their prayers are never answered.

III. *"I will be with him in trouble."*

Every heart knows its own bitterness. If the troubles that are represented by this audience could be written in a volume, it would take the biggest volume you have ever seen. We are apt to think that young people do not have any trouble, but if they haven't, there is one thing they can make sure of, that they are going to have trouble later. "Man is born unto trouble, as the sparks fly upward." Trouble is coming. No one is exempt. God has had one Son without sin, but He has never had one without sorrow. Jesus Christ, our Master, suffered as few men ever suffered, and He died very young. Ours is a path of sorrow and suffering, and it is so sweet to hear the Master say:

"I will be with you in trouble."

Don't let anyone think for a moment that you can get on without Him. You may say now, "I can get on; I am in good health and prosperity," but the hour is coming when you will need Him.

Many a Christian could bear witness to this point, that He has been with them in trouble, that in some dark hour when the billows seemed to be rolling up around them, they cried to Him, and He heard their cry, He answered their prayer, and He brought peace. There was joy in their sorrow, there was a star that lit up even the darkest night.

I remember being on that vessel, the *Spree,* when the shaft broke and a hole was knocked in her bottom out in mid-ocean, and the stern sank thirty feet. All my family but one was in Northfield, and I was making my way home, leaving friends in Europe. There I was in mid-ocean, pulled up, as it were, to look into my own grave for about forty-eight hours, without one ray of hope, humanly speaking. For forty-eight hours the burden was intense. My heart was like a lump of lead.

The accident happened Saturday morning. Sunday afternoon we had a prayer-meeting, and after prayer I read this ninety-first Psalm. If it had been let down from heaven, it could not have given more comfort. I went into my state room, and I fell on my knees, and I cried to the Lord:

"It is a time of trouble; help me."

And God took the burden. It rolled off, and I fell asleep. I never slept sounder than I did that night, and all the rest of the time. If a storm had burst on us any time during the week, we would have gone down, but God was with us in the time of trouble, and the burden was lifted.

A great many people seem to embalm their troubles. I always feel like running away when I see them coming. They bring out their old mummy, and tell you in a sad voice:

"You don't know the troubles I have!"

My friends, if you go to the Lord with your troubles, He will take them away. Would you not rather be with the Lord and get rid of your troubles, than be with your troubles and without God? Let trouble come if it will drive us nearer to God.

It is a great thing to have a place of resort in the time of trouble. How people get on without the God of the Bible is a mystery to me. If I didn't have such a refuge, a place to go and pour out my heart to God in such times, I don't know what I would do. It seems as if I would go out of my mind. But to think, when the heart is burdened, we can go and pour it into His ear, and then have the answer come back, "I will be with him," there is comfort in that!

I thank God for the old Book. I thank God for this old promise. It is as sweet and fresh to-day as it has ever been. Thank God, none of those promises are out of date, or grown stale. They are as fresh and vigorous and young and sweet as ever.

IV. *"I will honor him."*

"I will honor him." God's honor is something worth seeking. Man's honor doesn't amount to much. Suppose Moses had stopped down there in Egypt. He would have been loaded down with Egyptian titles, but they would never have reached us. Suppose he had been Chief Marshal of the whole Egyptian army, "General" Moses, "Commander" Moses; suppose he had reached the throne and become one of those Pharaohs, and his mummy had come down to our day. What is that compared with the honor God put upon him?

"I will honor him." Didn't God put honor on Moses? How his name shines on the page of history! The honor of this world doesn't last; it is transient; it is passing away, and I don't believe any man or woman is fit for God's service that is looking for worldly preferment, worldly honors and worldly fame. Let us get it under our feet, let us rise above it, and seek the honor that comes down from above.

V. *"With long life will I satisfy him."*

"With long life will I satisfy him." I get a good deal of comfort out of that promise. I don't think that means a short life down here, seventy years, eighty years, ninety years, or one hundred years. Do you think that any man living would be satisfied if they could live to be one hundred years old and then have to die? Not by a good deal. Suppose Adam had lived until to-day and had to die to-night, would he be satisfied? Not a bit of it! Not if he had lived a million years, and then had to die.

You know we are all the time coming to the end of things here, — the end of the week, the end of the month, the end of the year, the end of school days. It is end, end, end all the time. But, thank God, He is going to satisfy us with long life; no end to it, an endless life.

Life is very sweet. I never liked death; I like life. It would be a pretty dark world if death was eternal, and when our loved ones die we are to be eternally separated from them. Thank God, it is not so; we shall be re-united. It is just moving out of this house into a better one; stepping up higher, and living on and on forever.

There is a verse — probably you have never noticed it — that came to me with great sweetness some time ago. It is in the 21st Psalm, the 4th verse: "He asked life of thee, and thou gavest it him, even length of days forever and ever." Think of that, length of days *forever and ever!*

Do you think Moses is dead yet?

He never lived as he does to-day, never; and he is going to live on and on forever. What does Christ say? "If a man keep My saying, he shall never taste of death." Never!

Don't you want to live forever? You can if you will. Eternal life is as free as the air that you and I take into our lungs. "Verily, verily, I say unto you, He that heareth My word, and believeth on Him that sent Me, hath everlasting life, and shall not come into condemnation, but is passed from death unto life." Yes "I will satisfy him with long life."

Is there any one here who hasn't got eternal life? I don't like to pass over this, and leave any one outside the kingdom. If you are not in, my friends, take my advice; don't eat, or drink, or sleep until you get eternal life. Then this body may be taken away, but if it is, you will make something out of death. "If our earthly house of this tabernacle is dissolved, we have a building of God, an house not made with hands, eternal in the heavens."

When a young man, I was called upon suddenly, in Chicago, to preach a funeral sermon. A good many Chicago business men were to be there, and I said to myself,

"Now, it will be a good chance for me to preach the gospel to those men, and I will get one of Christ's funeral sermons."

I hunted all through the four Gospels trying to find one of Christ's funeral sermons, but I couldn't find one. I found He broke up every funeral He ever attended! He never preached a funeral sermon in the world. Death couldn't exist where He was. When the dead heard His voice they sprang to life. He will smash up the undertaking business when He comes to reign. "I am the resurrection and the life: he that believeth in Me, though he were dead, yet shall he live."

The 23d Psalm is more misquoted than anything else in the whole Bible. It is known in all the Catholic churches; it is known in the Greek church; it is in the Jewish synagogue; they chant it in a great many denominations, burying the dead; and armies went to battle chanting the 23d Psalm. And yet I believe it is more misquoted than anything in the Bible. People will weave it into their prayers, and conversation, and chapel services. They will say, "Yea, though I walk through the dark valley." They will always emphasize the word "dark," and send the cold chills running down your back. "Yea, though I walk through the *dark* valley of the shadow of death." I want to tell you, my dear friends, the word "dark" isn't there at all. The devil sticks that in there to confuse believers. It is, "Yea, though I walk through the valley of the shadow of death."

What is the difference?

Must not there be light where there is shadow? Can you get a shadow without light? If you doubt it, go down into the cellar to-night without a light, and find your shadow if you can. All that death can do to a true believer is to throw a shadow across his path. Shadows never hurt any one. You can walk right through shadows as you can through fog, and there is nothing to fear.

I pity down deep in my heart any man or woman that lives under the bondage of death! If you are under it, may God bring you out to-day! May you come right out into the liberty of the blessed gospel of the Son of God.

Jesus Christ came into the world to destroy death, and we can say with Paul, if we will, "Oh death, where is thy sting?" and we can hear a voice rolling down from heaven saying, "Buried in the bosom of the Son of God." He took death unto

His own bosom. He went into the grave to conquer and over-throw it, and when He arose from the dead said, 'Because I live, ye shall live also." Thank God, we have a long life with Christ in glory.

My dear friends, if we are in Christ we are never going to die. Do you believe that? If sometime you should read that D. L. Moody, of East Northfield, is dead, don't believe a word of it. He has gone up higher, that is all; gone out of this old clay tenement into a house that is immortal, a body that death cannot touch, that sin cannot taint, a body fashioned like unto His own glorious body. Moses wouldn't have changed the body he had at the transfiguration for the body he had at Pisgah. Elijah wouldn't have changed the body he had at the trans-figuration for the body he had under the juniper tree. They got better bodies; and I too am going to make something out of death.

VI. *"I will set him on high."*

"I will set him on high." God is able to do it. Up above the angels, up above the archangels, up above the cherubims and seraphims, on the throne with His own Son.

We are called to be sons and daughters of the eternal God. Do you know, the Prince of Wales cannot sit on the throne with Queen Victoria; they wouldn't allow it. The heir to the throne of Russia has just recently died, and they have appointed another to take his place, but he cannot sit on the throne with his brother, the Czar. But it is not so yonder. Christ has gone up and taken His seat at the right hand of the Father, and every son and daughter of God is to be lifted up onto the throne. My dear friends, think of the promise. Isn't it rich, isn't it sweet? "I will set him on high."

So that when our friends pass up to be on high and to be forever with Him, they are far better off.

VII. *"I will show him my salvation."*

"I will show him my salvation." That is a sweet promise. God can say to the angels — "Hark to that man that was once down in the depths, down in the gutter, but now he is lifted up and set upon my throne with my Son." Thank God for the riches of His grace in Christ Jesus!

I believe we don't learn the fringe of the subject of salvation down here. When our Master was on earth, He said He had many more things to say, but He could not reveal them to His disciples because they were not ready to receive them. But when we go yonder, where these mortal bodies have put on immortality, when our spiritual faculties are loosed from the thraldom of the flesh, I believe we shall be able to take more in. God will lead us from glory to glory, and show us the fullness of our salvation. Don't you think Moses knew more at the Mount of Transfiguration than he did at Pisgah? Didn't Christ talk with him then about the death He was to accomplish at Jerusalem? He couldn't have received this truth before, any more than the disciples, but when he had received his glorified body, Christ could show him everything.

BIBLIOGRAPHY

Biographical

Many have been issued, some during his life-time. After Moody's death in 1899 six were issued, mostly eulogistic. This was the prevailing mood during the first fifty years of this century, with the exception of a few more critical works. The following among many have been read and consulted and are mentioned as among the best.

1900.   Moody, W. R.: *The Life of Dwight L. Moody,* by his son. New York and London: Morgan and Scott, 1900; New York: Fleming H. Revell Co., 1900. This is the official authorized edition covering the major events of Moody's life and work. It is sympathetic and helpful, without historical perspective.

1930.   Moody, William R.: *D. L. Moody.* New York: Macmillan & Co. Moody's son wrote this second volume about his father. This is a new edition of the first, and is entirely rewritten. Many estimates of Moody had been made in the intervening years. The evangelist is now seen as an educator, and as a man of affection, yet judicious restraint.

1963.   Pollock, J. D.: *Moody:* A biographical portrait of the pacesetter in modern mass evangelism. New York: Macmillan Co., 1963. This more recent study is based upon careful enquiry into old records and papers now available to supplement earlier biographies. It is comprehensive, but not altogether setting Moody in the historical perspective, and is still somewhat eulogistic.

1969.   Findlay, James F. Jr.: *Dwight L. Moody: American Evangelist, 1837-1899.* Chicago and London: The University of Chicago Press, 1969. This is possibly the finest thus far of an attempted definitive study of Moody based upon research into all available data. It assesses both conservative and liberal points of view concerning him and evangelism. Now we see Moody within the context of the social, cultural, and theological ferment of his age with a sure place in American and British history.

Published Works of Moody

During Moody's lifetime newspapers reported his sermons and addresses verbatim. Later, enterprising religious leaders published selections in book form with sketches of his life and ministry. In this list appended there are some now out of print, and no attempt has been made to choose any selection from other edited works, only from those published under the name of Moody himself. Thus the bibliography is limited and selected for this *Treasury*.

Moody, D. L.: *Anecdotes*. New York: Fleming H. Revell Co., 1898

    Heaven. New York: Fleming H. Revell Co., 1880

    One Thousand and One Thoughts from My Library. New York: Fleming H. Revell Co., 1898

    Men of the Bible. New York: Fleming H. Revell Co., 1898

    Moody's Latest Sermons. Chicago: The Moody Press, 1900

    The Overcoming Life. New York: Fleming H. Revell Co., 1896

    Prevailing Prayer. New York. Fleming H. Revell Co., 1885

    Pleasure and Profit in Bible Study. New York: Fleming H. Revell Co., 1899

    Sowing and Reaping. New York: Fleming H. Revell Co., 1896

    Select Sermons. New York: Fleming H. Revell Co., 1881

    Secret Power. New York: Fleming H. Revell Co., 1881

    Short Talks. New York: Fleming H. Revell Co., 1900

    To the Work. New York: Fleming H. Revell Co., 1884

    Thoughts for the Quiet Hour. New York: Fleming H. Revell Co., 1900

    The Way to God. New York: Fleming H. Revell Co., 1864

    Weighed and Wanting. New York: Fleming H. Revell Co., 1898

Rhodes, R. S.: *Dwight Lyman Moody's Life, Work and Gospel Sermons*. Chicago: Rhodes and McClure Publishing Co., 1900

Simons, M. L.: *The Gospel Awakening* (Moody Sermons). Chicago: L. T. Palmer & Co., 1877

NOTES

The choice of these messages was based not upon the chronological sequence of their delivery, by Moody. A selection has been made by emphases and subjects to show the widespread nature of Moody's preaching.